Artificial Intelligence:
A 60 Minute Guide

Steven Finlay

Relativistic

Relativistic

e-mail: AI@relativistic.co.uk

ISBN-13: 978-1-9993253-5-0

ISBN-10: 1-9993253-5-4

To Sam and Ruby

Contents

Acknowledgements		vii
Foreword		xi
1.	What is Artificial Intelligence?	1
2.	Algorithms, Models and more Algorithms	13
3.	Neural Networks and Deep Learning	26
4.	The Impact of AI on Everyday Life	43
5.	The Changing Nature of Work	52
6.	Ethical AI?	64
7.	What Next?	75
Appendix A.	Further Reading	82
Appendix B.	Glossary	84
About the Author		100
Notes		102

Acknowledgements

I would like to thank my family, and my wife Samantha in particular, for their support in writing this book.

Foreword

About 60 minutes. That's the time it used to take my commuter train to travel from my home town of Preston to the great British city of Manchester. I found that this was an ideal time to catch up on my reading.

Having written several full-length books about artificial intelligence related topics, I thought that writing something about this fascinating subject, that could be read in a little over an hour, would be helpful for those who wanted to know more about artificial intelligence but without much time on their hands.

This book provides a concise, updated and abridged version of the material from some of my other books. If you are lucky enough to have read those, please don't buy this one! However, if you like this book, then you may like some of my other books too.

A fast reader can read at about 300 words a minute. With around 60 minutes to play with, that's about 18,000 words. To be honest, including preliminary matter and appendices, the total book is a bit longer than this. Therefore, it may take you a little bit longer than an hour, but I hope that the average reader is able to digest the main part of the book the allotted time.

Steven Finlay, July 2021.

1. What is Artificial Intelligence?

Barely a day goes by without another story about how Artificial Intelligence (AI) is changing our lives. This spans everything from how we work, travel and shop, to the way we obtain news and information to the gadgets in our homes. But what is artificial intelligence and where is it? It's supposed to be everywhere, but I never seem to meet any robots with whom I can have a meaningful discussion about it!

There isn't a standard definition of AI that everyone agrees with but a simple explanation is that a machine, that can act and reason just like a person, embodies everything it means to be artificially intelligent. This isn't an unreasonable place to start and leads one to envisage a world filled with human-like robots doing human-like things. In fact, the ability to replicate human behavior is a key feature of the famous "Turing test" devised by the mathematician Alan Turing[1].

In the test, a human judge converses with a human and a machine without knowing which is which. The judge can engage them in conversation about the weather, politics, the latest YouTube clip they'd seen or anything else they liked. The machine is considered intelligent if the judge is unable to identify which is the human and which is the machine.

There have been some very good efforts, but no machine has yet passed the Turing test and it'll probably be many years before a computer is able to do so convincingly and repeatedly[2].

The Turing test is interesting but has its limitations. In trying to pass the test, the focus has mainly been on fooling the judge rather than creating real intelligence. Those trying to pass the test haven't built a really excellent robot and then thought "I wonder if it'd be any good at the Turing test? Hey robot, do you want to give it a go?" Instead, they've considered what they need to do to pass the test and tried to build something that does that.

Another argument against the Turing test is that a machine doesn't need to be self-aware like people are to pass the test. It doesn't need to understand the responses it makes. It can pass by just blindly following some very clever computer code.

If we stick to the concept of a fully conscious self-aware thinking machine, with all the mental capabilities that we have, as our definition of artificial intelligence then we are years, if not decades, away from such machines. In fact, some argue that no system, based on the types of computers we use today, could ever be conscious as we understand it no matter how powerful they are. There is some additional (undiscovered) element required for human-like consciousness that can't be replicated via computation alone[3].

If we discard the requirement to be conscious and focus instead on the ability of computers to mimic the full spectrum of human intellectual capabilities, then there is nothing like this in the world today. This "Do it all" type of artificial intelligence, or *General AI* as it's often termed, is also likely to remain in the realms of science fiction for some time to come.

Fully human-like AI is a distant dream but don't be too disheartened. Instead of thinking of AI as something that must be like a person, let's lower the bar a little. If a machine can gather information and learn about a situation, and then decide upon a sensible course of action, then that's artificially intelligent behavior. More concisely, we can summarize this rather restricted definition of artificial intelligence as follows:

> Artificial Intelligence (AI) is the ability of a machine to assess a situation and then make an *informed decision* in pursuit of some *aim* or *objective*.

This definition encompasses both conscious and unconscious decision-making. An example of conscious human decision-making is where someone is deciding who would be the best candidate for a job. A machine capable of doing this instead of a hiring manager would qualify as intelligent within this area of expertise. An example of unconscious decision-making is looking at a picture and knowing that you are looking at a cat rather than a cake. Again, a machine that can do this would fall within our definition of artificial intelligence. Both of these examples of AI are in widespread use today.

In displaying intelligent behavior, a machine can make a decision on the basis of what it knows – an *informed decision*. If circumstances change; i.e. new information becomes available, then the machine will reassess the situation and a different decision may result. Introduce pictures of potatoes, and the object recognition system can learn to identify not just cats and cakes but potatoes as well.

If we look at the landscape today, there are lots of clever systems that satisfy this definition of AI. When you hear about some new application of artificial intelligence, this is pretty much the definition that is being referred to.

This definition of AI isn't one that all experts agree with, but from a practical perspective, it covers pretty much every tool, app and gadget that the tech companies describe as incorporating AI.

So, where is this type of limited AI being employed today? All over the place. Some common examples include:

- **Content detection.** These systems identify if text, pictures or speech relates to certain subjects. Social media companies use these tools to identify and remove offensive and/or illegal material posted to their sites so that you don't see them.

- **Chatbots.** Chatbots provide answers to peoples' questions. Simple chatbots are routinely used to automatically answer basic customer queries. More complex examples are personal digital assistants such as Amazon's Alexa and Google Assistant.

- **Streaming service recommendations.** Content providers, such as Netflix and Spotify, use AI tools to learn the preferences of individual users, and hence, the best song to play next or what programs to recommend.

- **Language translation**. Tools, such as Google Translate, are AI-driven apps that can translate almost any language into any other.

- **Policing and law enforcement.** One use is making parole decisions. The goal is to only recommend parole for prisoners with a low risk of reoffending. Another is using AI to help decide what areas to patrol to maximize arrest rates.

If you want to see some modern AI in action, then Microsoft's "CaptionBot" is a good place to start[4]. Upload a picture to the website and the AI software will describe what it sees. I found it quite fun because although it describes some images quite well, it sometimes gets things wrong or provides non-sensical answers. A picture of someone smoking was described as: "A man brushing his teeth" and a woman juggling prompted the reply: "I think it's a large white ball." Overall, it's quite an impressive app, but it's not without its limitations.

Another one to try is the thispersondoesnotexist[5] website. This generates pictures of people that look real but are completely artificial. The people in the photos don't exist!

AI is also moving beyond just assessing information and decision-making and more into the physical world; i.e. combining AI's decision-making capabilities with advances in engineering and robotics. This facilitates the automation of many physical tasks that would once have been undertaken or controlled by a person. Large warehouses are a prime example of a working environment that has seen a proliferation of robots in recent years with far less requirement for human staff to do things like stocking shelves or picking items for use/dispatch. If you want to see some examples of artificial intelligence combined with advanced robotics, then Boston Dynamics has lots of videos of their intelligent robots in action on their website[6].

All the aforementioned applications of artificial intelligence are examples of "*Weak AI*" or "*Narrow AI.*" These systems can be extraordinarily good at certain tasks, often better than the best human, but that's all they do. They can only make informed decisions about a narrow range of problems that they've been designed to deal with. If you want to use AI tech to do something else then you have to develop a new app from scratch.

Take object recognition systems, such as one used for the very important task of differentiating between cats, cakes and potatoes. The goal of the system is to correctly identify what object the camera is looking at. The AI has no other capability. It can't, for example, decide who is likely to be a good match for you on a dating site. Similarly, a tool such as Google Translate is fantastic at what it does, but will never be any use at detecting credit card fraud or deciding who's the best candidate for a job.

Another weakness of current state-of-the-art AI systems is that they can do some extraordinarily clever things, but they can also behave in unbelievably stupid ways if you take them just a short way outside of their comfort zone.

Today's best object recognition systems are better at identifying everyday objects than people are. However, engaging in a little mundane trickery, such as turning pictures through 90 degrees, can cause these systems to struggle[7]. Any normal person can recognize a bus that has rolled on its side, but many AI systems can't. Likewise, changing just a few pixels in an image, making no discernable changes that a person would notice, is enough to confuse them[8].

Microsoft's Tay chatbot provides another example of the limitations of current AI. Tay was designed to talk to teenagers on-line. Tay's developers don't seem to have considered the darker side of social media. Tay was withdrawn within hours because it started to tweet sexist, neo-Nazi and other inappropriate content[9]. Tay's designers didn't intend this but all Tay did was learn and adapt to conversational patterns it was exposed to. When people made inappropriate comments, Tay's programming just played them back in its own responses.

One lesson to learn from Tay is that current AI-based apps have no social awareness and no conscience. They just do what they've been tasked to do. Nothing more, nothing less. There's no angel sitting on their shoulder providing moral guidance.

This means that human expertise is required to moderate the outputs generated from many AI systems. This is to prevent the AI making decisions that would be illegal or unethical, or in some cases, just downright stupid.

One example of a human-defined ethical rule is a marketing AI that targets people with adverts for alcoholic drinks, such as gin. The AI may determine that some pregnant women are good targets. Targeting pregnant women is perfectly legal and some may want to drink gin (The Victorians didn't call it "Mother's ruin" without reason!). However, most people would agree that this is unethical because of the potential harm to the unborn child. Therefore, someone needs to ensure that the system also includes rules such as: "Don't target pregnant women" to over-ride any decision that the marketing AI might make. An example of a legal rule is not to promote adult products to children. A common sense rule is don't target dead people or prisoners with gin adverts.

There's been an explosion in AI-based apps recently, but what may be surprising is that commercial applications of AI aren't new. What may be the first commercial use of an AI technology was in credit granting. Before the 1950s, banks employed large teams of trained underwriters to decide who to grant credit to. They would weigh-up all the information they knew about someone and then decide if lending them money was a good idea. Every loan was manually assessed. Being an underwriter was an important and well paid job.

When commercial computers become available, lenders realized that they could use this new technology to assign loan applicants a probability of them defaulting on their loan, based on personal data such as their income, where they lived, what job they did and so on. These probabilities of default were branded "Credit scores." It was then a simple task to automate the credit scoring process to decide who to grant credit to on the basis of their score; i.e. grant loans to those with high credit scores and decline those with low scores.

What the banks realized was that these automated systems could outperform the best human underwriters. Credit scoring resulted in more good loans being granted and fewer bad ones. But that wasn't the end of the story. Humans were expensive and took several minutes to assess each loan application. Automated credit scoring was cheaper and took only a fraction of a second. The writing was on the wall for the underwriting profession.

These days, automated credit scoring rules the roost. Human underwriters do still exist, but they are a rare breed, who only assess loan applications in a very limited set of circumstances. For example, where a dispute arises and the law requires a human to review the original, machine-made, decision.

The credit scoring-based systems of the 1950s and 60s were very simple by today's standards. A modern AI practitioner (a **data scientist**) might laugh if you suggested that these systems constituted what they would call artificial intelligence. However, the idea of learning from large amounts of data, predicting outcomes and then making automated decisions on the basis of those predictions, are in principle, no different from the vast majority of AI applications in use today.

What has changed is the complexity of the systems that are now available. This is partly due to the "***Big Data***" world we now inhabit. With the advent of online shopping, smartphones and social media in the mid-late 2000s, there was an explosion in the amount of personal information available for AI-based systems to learn from. Similarly, there is now massive amounts of information about all sorts of business and industrial processes. Consequently, AI-based tools are being used to optimize processes in companies and factories around the world.

The second element fueling the rise of AI is the vast increase in cheap data storage and the computational power of modern computers under-pinned by some very clever algorithms (computer code). Much of the theory behind modern AI was developed decades ago, but it has only become feasible to deploy it with the availability of massive amounts of cheap computing power.

Things have also been helped immensely by the democratization of AI technologies. Not that long ago, if you wanted to play with AI software, then it would have cost thousands of dollars to buy it. These days, there are a whole host of (mostly free) software tools for developing AI applications on your laptop or home PC, or by using cloud services offered by the IT giants such as Microsoft[10] and Google[11]. If a home enthusiast wants to include voice recognition in the app they are developing, then they can just use the free version of the Alexa software that Amazon has made available[12].

Most of the tricky mathsy stuff has also been automated, meaning that you don't need to be a Nobel prize winner or mathsy PhD to build an AI-based application. Anyone who is numerate, with some basic computer programming skills, can start producing basic AI-driven apps very quickly.

When talking about artificial intelligence, you will almost invariably come across the term *Machine Learning*. In a sentence:

> Machine learning is the use of mathematical procedures to analyze and infer things from data.

Machine learning aims to discover useful things about the relationships between different bits of information. In particular, correlations between one thing and another. Some examples of individual correlations are:

- More children are born in Spring than in Autumn.

- High income households tend to consume more beef than lower income households.

- Asthma is more prevalent amongst city dwellers than country folk.

It's important to appreciate the difference between *correlation* and *causation*. We aren't saying that Spring causes more births or that a high income leads to eating more beef. All we are saying is that when we see a change in one thing we also see a change in another. If two things are correlated it doesn't necessarily follow that one causes the other to happen.

Once the relationships (patterns or correlations) have been identified, then these relationships can be used to infer the behavior of new cases when they present themselves. The more information available the more accurate and nuanced the inferences about the various relationships becomes. To put it another way, the more data you feed machine learning with, the better it becomes at figuring out what is going on.

In essence, this is analogous to the way you and I learn. As we gather more information from observing what goes on around us, the better we become at drawing conclusions about how the world works.

Where machine learning comes into its own is when there are many subtle correlations between lots of different, sometimes seemingly unrelated, things and a particular outcome or behavior. A doctor may be able to assess five or six different factors when making a diagnosis. However, a machine learning-based system can consider thousands of correlations between different data items and different medical conditions all at the same time.

When machine learning is applied to vast quantities of personal data, this translates into systems that can predict how people are expected to behave in the future. Having identified the relationships that exist, and given detailed information about a someone, it's possible to predict their future behavior very accurately. A machine that can predict what you are going to do? – scary? Yes, but not half as scary as a government or corporation that has control of that machine and what it may try and make you do on the basis of those predictions.

When an organization such as YouTube or Facebook uses an AI-driven marketing app to decide what ads to show you, this is based on the analysis of millions of people's characteristics such as their location, browsing history, the content of their posts on social media and what they subsequently bought. This model of purchasing behavior is applied to you and your set of characteristics, right now, to predict what you are likely to buy next, and hence, what ads you should see. As things about you change the predictions are updated, and consequently, a different set of products may be presented to you.

Returning to credit scoring, things are very similar. Loan companies apply machine learning to historic loan agreements to identify features of good paying customers. It may find, for example, that older people are best at paying back their loans or that accountants tend to be worse than school teachers. Once the relationships in the data have been identified, these can be used to calculate your credit score. Your credit score is, in effect, a prediction as to how likely you are to repay your debts in the future.

An important feature of the machine learning process is that it considers all of the different information it knows about you in combination, not in isolation. Everybody is treated individually and the credit score you receive is based on a completely different combination of characteristics than everyone else. Your credit score is unique to you[13].

More widely, all the applications of AI discussed so far are based on similar machine learning principles. A hiring AI, used to identify good job candidates predicts, for each candidate, how likely it is that they will be a good fit for the role. An AI-based object recognition system creates predictions as to how likely it is that the pattern of pixels it's presented with is relates to each object. If the system predicts that there is a 5% chance that the image is a cat, a 15% chance that it's a cake and an 80% chance it's a potato, then the system will report that it sees a potato.

Advanced game playing AI technologies also apply this approach. Each turn, a chess playing AI assigns each possible move a probability of leading to checkmate. It then selects the move most likely to move it towards that state. These probabilities have been derived based on large numbers of historic games and how those games played out based on the moves that were made.

Technically, machine learning and artificial intelligence are not the same thing. Artificial intelligence is a much broader field of study. Practically however, nearly every commercial AI application in the world today has some form of machine learning at its heart. It's perhaps not surprising that many people use the terms "Artificial intelligence" and "Machine learning" interchangeably, even if it's not quite right to do so.

Another way to think about this is that machine learning is one very powerful tool that can be used in the creation of AI powered apps, gadgets and robots, but it's not AI itself. There are other aspects to artificial intelligence that machine learning doesn't cover and there are other tools available that can be used to develop AI applications, such as **Expert Systems** and **Evolutionary Computing**. However, machine learning is driving nearly all real-world AI applications in the world today.

2. Algorithms, Models and more Algorithms

Algorithms underpin all modern AI applications. They can be very complex, but at its heart, an ***algorithm*** is just a set of actions, performed one after another, to complete a given task. Almost any activity can be described using an algorithm. The following algorithm describes how I make tea.

---

1. Put a teabag in a cup.
2. Boil some water.
3. Fill the cup with hot water.
4. Wait a few minutes for the tea to brew.
5. Take the teabag out.
6. Add milk and sugar to taste.
7. The tea is now ready.
8. END of algorithm (now drink the tea!)

As you can see, my tea making algorithm isn't difficult to understand. The algorithm captures how I make tea but you may do things differently. Maybe you use loose leaf and a fancy teapot. Or are you're a bit of a slob who leaves their teabag in the cup as they drink it? Many variants are possible, each with their own benefits and drawbacks. Some algorithms are more efficient, others faster, others more flexible. They all approach the problem in a different way.

When it comes to computer algorithms, the language isn't English like in the tea making example. A more stylized and precise language is used that a computer can understand – computer code. If I rewrote the tea making algorithm to be a bit more like computer code, then it would be more along the following lines:

1. Get 1 cup, with a capacity of between 0.30 and 0.40 litres.
2. Put 1 teabag in the cup.
3. Get kettle.
4. Empty kettle (of any old water).
5. Fill kettle with 0.25 litres of cold water from kitchen tap.
6. Turn kettle on.
7. Heat kettle until water boils.
8. Turn kettle off.
9. Pour the water from the kettle into the cup.
10. Wait for 3 minutes.
11. Remove the teabag from the cup.
12. IF milk required THEN add 25 ml of milk (0.025 litres).
13. IF sugar required THEN add 15 grams of sugar.
14. END of Algorithm.

Now, this isn't proper computer code, but hopefully it demonstrates my point. Everything needs to be clear and exact. It's obvious to us that you just fill the cup until nearly full, leaving space for milk if required. That's all we need to know to complete the task. Our innate common sense provides the rest. For a computer, unless you specify exact sizes and quantities you'll get into trouble. If instruction 7 said "Heat water to 100C" instead of "Until boils" then the algorithm would never finish unless it was working at sea level. Above sea level, the kettle would boil dry because the water would never reach 100C.

The boiling point of water drops significantly once you are just a few hundred meters above sea level[14].

OK. Now we know what an algorithm is, let's get back to AI and machine learning where several types of algorithms are applied in a number of different ways. Consider Figure 1.

Figure 1. Algorithms used in an AI application.

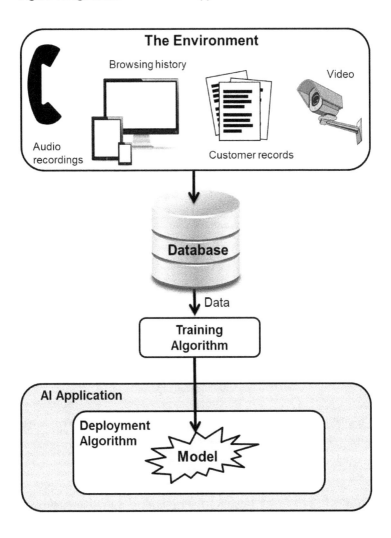

First, data about the environment (***training data***) is collected together, as represented by the database in Figure 1. Once we have data, we can start to apply the algorithms. There are three types of algorithm involved with a typical AI application.

1. **Training Algorithms.** These learn about the environment from the training data. In particular, how one environmental factor is influenced by all the others. The resulting ***model*** captures the relationships that have been found.

2. **Models.** The model produced by the training algorithm is itself a type of algorithm that contains a record of the relationships that the training algorithm has discovered.

3. **Deployment Algorithms.** These provide the operational framework to enable models to used.

The training algorithm is usually the most complex part of the process but it's just a means to an end. Once we have a model then we don't need the training algorithm any more (at least not until we want to build another model).

How does a model produce predictions or other outputs? A model is set of equations that captures how the environment changes under a given set of circumstances[15]. When provided with inputs, the model processes these and produces outputs. The outputs describe what the inputs mean in relation to some objective that the system has. To put things into context, let's consider some real-world examples. However, rather jumping straight to the real cutting-edge stuff, let's begin with some mundane and somewhat old school examples.

Let's say that our objective is to develop a model to identify people at risk of developing heart disease. They can then be targeted to try and reduce their risk of developing the disease in the future.

The environmental data that the training algorithm is going to use is a database of thousands of medical records from several years ago. Each patient record is labelled to indicate which patients subsequently developed heart disease in the years that followed.

The training algorithm trawls through the patient data looking for all the things that are correlated with developing heart disease. The relationships found by the training algorithm are captured by the model at the end of the process, as shown in Figure 2.

Figure 2. A decision tree model for heart disease.

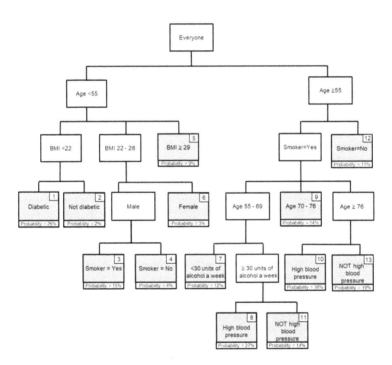

This type of model is called a ***Decision Tree***. The algorithm that derived the decision tree may have been very complex, but the way the decision tree model works is pretty simple. You simply start at the top of the tree and work your way down until there is nowhere else to go. The final "leaf node" into which a patient falls drives a single output: The probability of developing heart disease. From Figure 2, for a 47-year-old female with a Body Mass Index (BMI) of 27[16], the predicted probability of them getting heart disease is 3%

Anyone can understand and use a decision tree model like this. However, the real magic happens when we deploy the model in a doctor's surgery. The doctor can present the model with up-to-date medical records for all of their thousands of patients *without* heart disease today. The model then generates a probability of each patient developing heart disease in the future based on the leaf node of the decision tree into which they fall.

This is a very powerful thing to be able to do. In a world where healthcare resources are limited, those the model predicts have the highest chance of developing heart disease can be targeted for individual help. The doctor might decide that they have enough free time to invite all patients who fall into leaf nodes 1 and 10 to attend a lifestyle review because these people have the highest chance of developing the disease. If someone ends up in node 1 or 10 it's not guaranteed that they'll develop heart disease, but their chance of doing so is higher than everyone else.

Because it's all on a computer, the patients can be regularly reassessed, and if their chance of getting heart disease increases, they can be added to the contact list for an appointment. Things become even more interesting when we start adding information, not traditionally held in medical records, such as biometric data from smart watches and people's grocery shopping. This type of rapidly changing real-time data often provides huge insights into people's behavior in all sorts of different ways including their health.

Let's now return to the world of credit scoring. Imagine a bank that wants to build an "AI-driven underwriting app." Customers will use this phone-based app to apply for loans and it will automatically decide if they are creditworthy enough to be granted one.

The bank has a database containing information about

thousands loans it granted in the past. This database contains two types of information that are going to be very important for developing the underwriting app.

1. **Application data.** This is information about peoples' loan applications. This includes stuff they provided themselves, such as their age and employment status but also lots of other information such as credit history from a credit reference agency and social media data.

2. **Repayment data.** This is information about loan repayments. In particular, did the customer repay their debt or did they default?

The aim/objective is to use the application data to predict their chance of defaulting if we decide to lend them the money.

To produce a model of the underwriting environment, a suitable training algorithm is applied to the loan data. This is having first set up the algorithm such that it knows that the objective is to predict repayment behavior. The algorithm then trawls through all of the historic loan data to establish which items are predictive of loan repayment behavior and in what way.

The result is a ***Scorecard*** type model, as shown in Figure 3.

To produce the scorecard, the training algorithm examined all the data it was presented with. This may have included thousands of data items but the algorithm concluded that only 8 items, as shown in Figure 3, are important for assessing credit risk.

This isn't unusual. Often, only a fraction of the data is useful but you don't know what's important in advance. The algorithm must analyze everything if you want the model to be as accurate as possible. There may have been information about marital status, qualifications, people's tweets etc., but these weren't found to be important predictors of repayment behavior.

Figure 3. A scorecard model.

Starting score	700
1. Annual income	
<= $25,000	-21
$25,001 - $30,000	-14
$30,001 - $40,000	-9
$40,001 - $60,000	0
$60,001 - $85,000	5
$85,001 - $120,000	9
$120,001 - $160,000	25
> $160,000	32
2. Employment status	
Unemployed	-42
Full-time or retired	28
Part-time	7
Homemaker	28
Student	-8
3. Time in current employment	
Not in full or part-time employment	-14
<1 year	-25
1 - 2 years	-10
3 - 8 years	0
> 8 years	31
4. Eye color	
Blue	4
Green	0
Brown	-3
Other	0
5. Residential status	
Home owner	26
Renting	12
Living with parent	0
6. Number of credit cards	
0	-17
1 - 2	0
3 - 4	-5
5 - 7	-11
8+	-24
7. In arrears with any existing credit agreements?	
Yes	-38
No	0
8. Bankrupt?	
Yes	-62
No	0

If you want to calculate your credit score, just add and subtract the values that apply using the following algorithm:

1. Give yourself the starting score of 700.
2. Add to this all the other scores that apply to you.
3. Hey presto, that's your credit score.
4. END of algorithm.

So, for someone with the following attributes:

5. Has an annual income of $38,000.
6. Is in full-time employment.
7. Has been in their current employment for 2 years.
8. Has green eyes.
9. Is a home owner.
10. Has two credit cards.
11. Is not in arrears with any existing credit agreements.
12. Is not bankrupt.

They start with 700. 9 points are subtracted due to their income, 28 points added for their employment status and so on to get a final score of 735. The higher the score, the more creditworthy you are; i.e. the more likely you are to repay any money you borrow.

The strength of the relationships are reflected in the magnitude of the scores. If one attribute has a larger score than another, then that indicates that it's more predictive and contributes more to the final score that someone receives.

Many things in the scorecard align with common sense. If someone hasn't been in their job very long or has recently been declared bankrupt then it's reasonable to assume that they aren't as financially stable as people on high incomes or who've been in their job a long time. Therefore, they get lower scores to reflect the increased risk that they represent.

Why can't I just get an experienced underwriter to come up with a scorecard based on their expert opinion? Why do I need an algorithm? Well you could, but there are two things that tend to result in scorecards derived using algorithms being better than those derived by human experts[17].

First, the scores assigned to each attribute are optimal. They are as good as they can be, based on the training data. Giving someone -42 for being unemployed is better than giving them -41 or -43 because that best reflects the risk from being unemployed. Second, the algorithm can find completely unexpected relationships in the data that an underwriter may not have considered important.

In this example, the unexpected thing is eye color. People with blue eyes are a better credit risk than people with other eye colors. This brings us on to a very important danger that exists when machine learning training algorithms are applied. All they do is find relationships in data. They don't have any insight into the meaning of that data, why those relationships exist or the context within which the data was collected.

Eye color predicts creditworthiness but it's also correlated with ethnicity. Historically, there's been a lot of prejudicial bias against certain ethnicities which may be reflected in the training data. It's therefore ethically questionable to include eye color in a predictive model used for this type of commercial purpose. Some might argue that removing eye color from the scorecard will reduce its accuracy, and they would be right, but that's the price one pays to ensure that the model is fair, and in many regions of the world, legal too.

A credit score is a measure of creditworthiness but how does an organization use the scorecard? How does it decide what a good or bad credit score is, and most importantly, how high do you have to score to get a loan?

Imagine that I now calculate credit scores for the thousands of customers that previously had a loan. I can then use the scores, in conjunction with the information about loan repayment behavior, to generate a customer score profile as shown in Figure 4.

Figure 4. Interpreting model scores.

Score Range	Percent of customers who repaid their loans	Percent of customers who defaulted
0 - 550	55%	45%
551 - 600	77%	23%
601 - 650	83%	17%
651 - 700	88%	12%
701 - 750	91%	9%
751 - 800	96%	4%
801 or more	99%	1%

In Figure 4, the leftmost column shows the score range and the rightmost column the proportion of people who subsequently defaulted on their loan. For the customer who scored 735, they fall into the 701 – 750 category where 9% of customers defaulted on their loans in the past. From that, we estimate that our customer, applying for a new loan today, also has a 9% chance of defaulting if we grant them a loan[18].

In retail credit, every loan company operates at different levels of profitability. Each has its own view as to what chance of defaulting is acceptable. Let's say, that in this example, the loan company can make a profit on people whose probability of default is 14% or less. The *decision rule* or *threshold* to apply is simply:

- Grant loans to applicants scoring 651 or more.

- Decline loans to applicants scoring less than 651.

So, our customer who scored 735, with a predicted 9% chance of defaulting, is deemed an acceptable risk and will be granted the loan.

That's a very simple example but the idea of having a threshold, or cut-off, is fundamental to all sorts of AI applications. If the model output (the score) is above a certain value do one thing, if it's below a certain value do something else.

A key feature of these types of models is that the process can incorporate adaptation and continuous improvement. The model can be updated automatically, in real-time, whenever new data becomes available. The more data available, the more predictive the model becomes.

Scorecard and decision tree models are used all over the place. I've even seen a scorecard used in A&E to support amputation decisions. Score high enough and they cut it off! However, they do have their weaknesses. In particular, they aren't always as good as people when they are applied to tasks where:

1. There is a lot of data available that contains very complex, nuanced and inter-dependent relationships within the data.

2. They are used to predict multiple complex outcomes. For both the heart disease and credit scoring models, there was only one output predicting a single thing (getting heart disease and loan repayment respectively).

In the past, when what little data did exist tended to be in a neat, structured, tabular format, like in a spreadsheet such as Microsoft

Excel, this wasn't so much of a problem. However, in todays' world, we are awash with data. As the amount and variety of data has grown, even the best algorithms for producing scorecard and decision tree type models struggle to deliver good solutions. Some examples of complex tasks it has proven very hard to get good results for using scorecard and decision tree type models include:

- Playing games. This includes traditional games such as chess and Go, as well as computer games like StarCraft and Quake.

- Identifying and describing items contained in pictures.

- Speech recognition and language translation.

- Creating advertising copy; i.e. writing text to promote a product or service when you look it up online.

To be able to equal or exceed human abilities in these fields, something more flexible, more adaptive and just downright more powerful is required. Something biologically inspired...

3. Neural Networks and Deep Learning

Billions of neurons with trillions of connections between them. That's what drives our intelligence and our ability to learn and adapt when we encounter something new.

Back in the 1950s, scientists first developed the concept of an artificial neuron[19] that simulated, very simplistically, the behavior of biological neurons. Later, the idea of linking several artificial neurons together, to create a *neural network*[20], was proposed as a way to represent complex problems[21]. However, it has only been in the last few years that the necessary computing capabilities have become readily available to allow their full potential to be realized. Today, advanced neural networks models are at the cutting edge of artificial intelligence and machine learning research.

The first thing to say about neural network models is that they are often touted as being immensely complex "Brain like" things, but they can be readily understood if you are willing to spend a little time and effort studying them. A typical neural network is much more complex than the scorecards and decision trees introduced in the previous chapter but the underlying principles are not much different. There's just a lot more of it.

To show how a neural network works, let's start with the basic building block of a neural network – the *neuron*. Figure 5 illustrates how an artificial neuron works, based on the credit scoring example introduced in the previous chapter.

Figure 5. An artificial neuron.

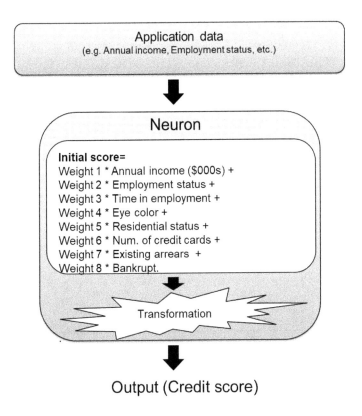

The neuron in Figure 5 works as follows:

1. Application data provides the inputs to the neuron. This is just like in the scorecard and decision tree models.

2. Each input is multiplied by a weight[22].

3. The resulting values are added together to get an initial score.

4. The initial score is transformed to lie within a certain range[23], often between 0 and 1. This is so that when several neurons

are combined to produce a neural network all the neurons produce values in the same range.

5. The transformed version of the initial score is the output produced by the neuron; i.e. the credit score.

An artificial neuron isn't mysterious or complex. It isn't really that much different from the scorecard model introduced in the last chapter[24]. The main difference is the transformation to force the neuron's score to lie in a fixed range. To produce a neural network several neurons are connected together, as shown in Figure 6.

Figure 6. A neural network model.

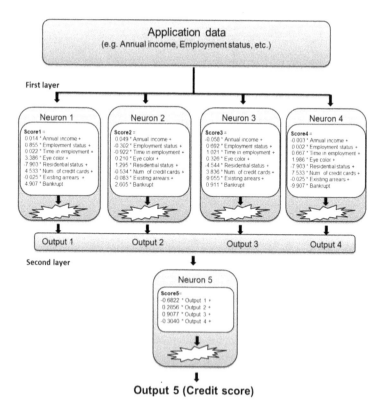

In Figure 6, the Credit Score (Output 5) from the network is calculated as follows:

1. The application data is supplied separately to each of the four neurons in the first layer.

2. Each neuron has its own weights. The weights, when combined with the application data, create scores (Score1, Score2, etc.)

3. The scores are transformed to produce four outputs.

4. The four outputs provide the inputs to the single neuron in the second layer (Neuron 5).

5. Neuron 5 combines the inputs with a further set of weights to create Score5.

6. Score5 is transformed to create the final credit score. [25]

The collection of weights in the network represent the patterns identified by the *training algorithm*. If you want a biological analogy, the weights can be thought of as a memory of the learning that has taken place that can be recalled whenever you want to make another credit scoring decision.

How does the training algorithm determine what the weights should be? Many different algorithms can be used to find the weights in a neural network, but they all tend to adopt the following principles:

1. Assign each weight a random or zero value.

2. Calculate the scores generated by the network for all cases in the training data.

3. Assess the model's accuracy; e.g. for the credit scoring model, how well it assigns high scores to good paying customers and low scores to defaulters.

4. Adjust the weights to improve the model's accuracy. For the credit scoring example, so that more good payers get higher scores and more bad payers get lower scores.

5. Repeat steps 1-4 until no further significant improvement in model accuracy is observed.

The complex math occurs in Step 4. This process of adjusting the weights is called *training*. A simple training approach is to randomly try different values and see what works best. However, this is very inefficient. Even the most powerful computer could run for years and still not find a good model using this approach. In practice, neural network training algorithms are cleverer than this. They adopt different weight adjustment strategies based on the model's performance between each iteration of the algorithm. The algorithm terminates when further adjustments deliver no significant improvement in model accuracy.

One reason neural networks are popular is that they are often better than scorecards and decisions trees at spotting subtle patterns in the training data. Their main drawback is that their outputs are not intuitive. You may know what all the weights are and understand how the final score is calculated. However, if I asked you which of the inputs in Figure 6 contribute most to the final score, then that's far less obvious than with the scorecard model (Figure 3). This can be a problem if there is a business or legal requirement to explain how the model score was arrived at.

Deep learning is the latest evolution of neural networks. The network in Figure 6 has two layers of neurons but there is no reason why there can't be more layers, as illustrated in Figure 7.

Figure 7. A deep neural network.

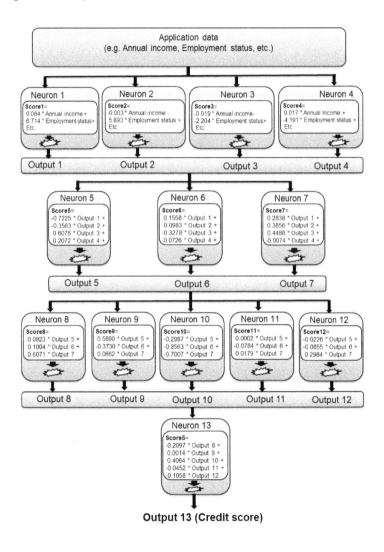

Output 13 (Credit score)

The two models take exactly the same input data and deliver the same type of output. However, the network in Figure 7 has 2 extra layers of neurons. What you tend to find is that as more layers are added, so the ability of the network to identify complex patterns increases. The more layers the deeper the network.

The networks in Figures 6 and 7 have a single neuron in the final layer that generates a single credit score. Another big strength of neural networks is that they can be structured to have more than one output. This is important for tasks where there can be thousands of options to choose from, each requiring a separate output.

Returning to our object recognition task, let's think about how a neural network might be structured to identify objects in a picture. As before, we need to gather lots of environmental information for the training algorithm to use. In this case, let's assume that the training data contains several thousand pictures of cats, cakes and potatoes as follows:

- **Input data.** Each pixel in a picture is represented by four pieces of data. A red, blue and yellow component to indicate the colour of the pixel, plus a value to represent the intensity (brightness) of the pixel.

- **Category data.** Each image is labelled to indicate if it contains a picture of a cat, a cake or a potato.

The objective is to use the input data to predict the category of object in the picture (cat, cake or potato). A neural network model like this could have millions of inputs, one for each pixel element, thousands upon thousands of neurons spread across a dozen or more layers, and 3 outputs as illustrated in Figure 8.

Figure 8. A neural network model for object recognition.

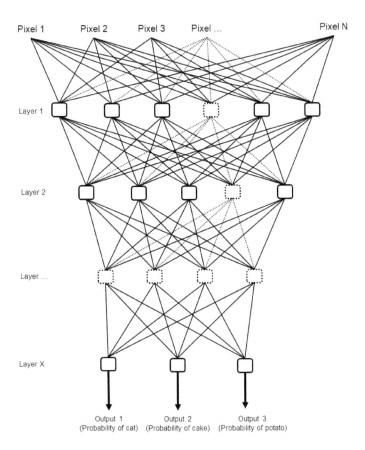

Pixel 1   Pixel 2   Pixel 3   Pixel ...   Pixel N

Layer 1

Layer 2

Layer ...

Layer X

Output 1   Output 2   Output 3
(Probability of cat) (Probability of cake) (Probability of potato)

In Figure 8, each output represents the probability that the image is either a cat, cake or potato respectively.

After training, when you present the network with a completely new image, the pixels representing the image are processed through the network. Then, you simply compare the 3 outputs and select the one that has the highest probability. If output 1 gives a 5% chance that the image is a cat, output 2 a 15% chance it's a cake and output 3 an 80% chance it's a potato, then the conclusion is it's a picture of a potato.

If we want a more general system, that can identify many more everyday objects, then the same principles apply. It's just a case of having enough images to train a suitably structured network with.

Other avenues of research associated with deep learning consider how the neurons in the network are connected. For example, you can include feedback loops so that the outputs of neurons in later layers act as inputs to earlier layers, which is called a **recurrent neural network**. This makes it possible to incorporate a representation of time or event ordering. Text prediction (like you get on your phone) is one such example. The word order so far is a key factor in predicting what word comes next. Another approach is to create sparse networks (**convoluted networks**) that contain relatively few connections between the neurons in different layers. This can help reduce the computing power required for certain types of problem[26].

One recent advance in deep neural networks are **General Adversarial Networks** or GANs, where two neural networks compete with each other to generate new and original content[27].

Let's say, that we want to produce a neural network that can create artificial pictures of people. They look just like real people but the people don't actually exist. Why would you want to do this? Maybe it's just for a bit of fun, but maybe you want to use the pictures in advertising or on virtual catwalks so that you don't need get the permission of real people to use their images and so on.

We start with two untrained neural networks models. For arguments sake, let's call the first neural network "The Judge." And the second "The Student."

The Judge assesses images it's presented with and decides if the images are of real people or something else. The Judge has a single output that represents the probability that the image is real. In principle, the Judge works just like any of the other models we've discussed previously. If the model output is more than 50%, then we guess that image is real otherwise we assume it's artificial.

Now, let's think about the Student. The Student's goal is to create realistic pictures of people. The Student is doing its job well if it can fool the Judge; i.e. it creates fake pictures that the Judge assigns a 50%+ probability of it being a real person.

The Student model is sort of back-to-front. With a normal object recognition system, the inputs to the model are a set of pixels and the output a set of probabilities (Like Figure 8). With the Student however, the outputs from the model are a set of pixels. The inputs are a set of random numbers[28].

First, we train the Judge using images that are labelled to indicate if they are of real people or something else. Once this initial training is complete, then the Judge is pretty good at identify images of people.

Returning to the Student, the model weights are initially chosen at random. The result? A set of meaningless images of random dots. These are presented to the Judge to assess, which has no problem identifying all the images as fake; i.e. it assigns them very low probabilities of being real.

The probabilities generated by the Judge are fed back to the Student and the training algorithm adjusts the model weights so as to produce a better set of images next time round. The algorithm used to train the Judge is also rerun. However, this time, the training data also includes the images generated by the Student.

This process is repeated many times, with each network continually learning from the outputs of the other. Eventually, a status quo is reached. The Student produces images of people that look real. As far as the Judge can tell, they are real, even though they are completely artificial. This is how the images on the thispersondoesnotexist[29] site are created.

Creative opportunities for GANs are vast. Amazon, for example, is reported to be using GANs to design garments by using images of fashionable clothing to train it to produce new designs that have similar stylistic features but which are completely original[30].

Likewise, for music and other creative works.

GANs show huge promise, but the potential for misuse is also extensive. In particular, it's driving many of the "Deepfake" stories, being reported in the press, to create fake media recordings of politicians and other famous people.

Why are neural network models so good at what they do? How do they manage to capture the nuances of complex problems leading to better judgements than the best human experts? One way to think about this is that learning to play a game like chess or Go is analogous to mapping an unknown landscape that the training algorithm explores as it goes. The model weights capture the features of the landscape and how one gets from one part of the landscape to another using different actions (game moves).

In mapping the features of a game, the training algorithms find parts of the landscape that people haven't explored before as well as new (better or more efficient) routes for travelling between one point and another. In effect, they have discovered new styles of play that have never been seen by human players before.

It has been argued that in finding these new styles of play the neural networks have displayed non-human i.e. alien, intelligence. However, another perspective is that it's not a new way of thinking, but rather the training algorithms have found new features and patterns that humans have just not got around to thinking about yet. It doesn't necessarily mean that the network is displaying a different type of thinking altogether, but instead, the training algorithm has found a new area of the landscape to explore that people have not yet reached.

This principle of mapping and exploration also applies in other application domains, not just games. One example is supporting scientific discovery, particularly in areas of research where huge numbers of possibilities have to be explored to find useful solutions – needle in haystack type problems.

A classic needle in a haystack problem is predicting the 3D structures of complex molecules such as proteins[31]. There are trillions of possible protein molecules, but only a handful have any practical applications. Being able to determine the likely shape of a molecule from its component parts means it's much easier to identify which molecules are likely to be useful and which are not.

What's amazing about machine learning models, and deep neural network models in particular, is that they can be trained to predict almost any outcome imaginable to a degree that equals or exceeds the best human decision-makers *if* sufficient good quality information (training data) is available. Want to predict the outcome of baseball or soccer games? Then feed the training algorithm with data about historic games and a well-designed model will be beat the best human pundits. Want a tool that decides which stocks to buy? then better to trust a machine learning model than a stock broker. Want to optimize the layout of a factory or supermarket? Then there are neural network algorithms that can do that better than any human could.

All of the different ways of building models that we've discussed so far have assumed that there is a database containing data about the environment, which includes details about the thing you want to infer (predict). If we think about the tasks we've considered so far:

- When building the decision tree model to predict heart disease (Figure 2) patients' medical record were flagged to indicate which developed heart disease.

- When creating the scorecard and neural network models for credit scoring (Figures 3, 6 and 7), each loan application was matched to data about loan repayment.

- When talking about using a deep neural network to identify images, each image in the training data was tagged to indicate if the image was of a cat, cake or potato.

For all of these tasks the training data was labelled to indicate what the outcome was in each case. This type of machine learning, using labelled training data, is called *supervised learning*.

Most real-world AI-based applications, such as target marketing, voice recognition and employee vetting are examples of supervised learning. However, there are times when there isn't any labelled data for the training algorithm to use. In these situations, a different set of techniques, referred to as *unsupervised learning,* can be applied.

The most common type of unsupervised learning in use today is *clustering*[32]. Clustering algorithms are based on the principle of minimizing the *distance* between cases in the training data. This doesn't necessarily mean physical distance, but how similar cases are in terms of specific data items. The distance between two people aged 23 and 25 is less than that between people aged 17 and 76. If we are talking about smoking, then two smokers have a distance of zero whereas a smoker and a non-smoker don't and so on.

With clustering, a model isn't produced at the end of the process, which means it can't be used to generate predictions about how individual cases are going to behave. There is just an identifier to say which cluster an observation belongs to. You are in cluster 9 whereas I've been assigned to cluster 4, for example.

Customer profiling to group similar people together is one of the best-known applications of clustering, but clustering approaches are also being applied successfully to many other tasks such as document clustering. In fields such as law and academic research, there is a requirement to regularly trawl through the ever-growing pile of published literature to find information relating to certain cases or types of research. In medicine, for example, almost a million academic papers are published each year[33]. Documents are grouped (clustered) together based on how similar they are in terms of subject matter, writing style, word count and a host of other features.

Document clustering can also be applied to tweets, newsfeeds, blog posts and other rapidly changing media in real time. Pictures and video can also be categorized in a similar way. News organizations use these approaches to automatically flag new posts about specific topics as they appear. They can then include them in their own media publications almost immediately. Social media companies and governments use similar methods (as well as predictive models) to identify illegal or undesirable content.

Supervised learning work well when there is a large amount of labelled data. If there are no labels available, then unsupervised learning, such as clustering, can sometimes prove useful; albeit in a somewhat different context. There are however, situations where there may be no data initially, but the learning process is able to assess its performance on a case-by-case basis as it goes. The model is adjusted each time, based on some measure of success or reward that is calculated each time a task is attempted. This type of machine learning is called *reinforcement learning*.

Data scientists often talk about three distinct types of machine learning; i.e. supervised, unsupervised and reinforcement learning. However, reinforcement learning shares many features with supervised learning. In particular, it delivers a model, typically based on some form of neural network. The key difference is that it generates training data as it goes, rather than using pre-existing training data to derive the final model.

A great example of the difference between supervised and reinforcement learning is how model training occurs to create a chess playing program. A supervised approach would take thousands of game moves (or sequence of moves) from previously played games as the observation data, with the labelled outcome data providing an indication of if the move was a good one or not. The scores produced by the model are used to indicate which piece to move and to where. The algorithm then finds the model weights that result in the overall best set of moves, measured against the moves contained in the development sample.

With reinforcement learning, no data is provided initially – none at all! The model scores still indicate which move to make just like the supervised approach. However, initially these will be more or less random, given that there isn't any training data. Each time a move is made the status of the board (the new state of being) is re-evaluated. The algorithm then adjusts the weights in the model based on how successful its move was deemed to be.

Evaluating how successful a move is in chess is complex and will often incorporate probable future states of being as well as the current one. However, for the purposes of this example, a simple success criteria is the difference in the value of each players' pieces remaining on the board after a move has been made[34]. If your move results in the taking of a high value piece, but not losing one yourself, then that's a strong success. Making a move and then having one of your pieces taken is a failure, yielding a low measure of success. The ultimate success or failure is losing one's king – checkmate. In this way, by assessing each move and adjusting the model weights accordingly, the program learns by itself without needing to be supplied with any prior information.

An advantage of reinforcement learning is that there's no limit to the set of moves that can be explored as the training algorithm progresses. With supervised learning, you are limited to the labelled examples in the training data. For a game like chess, even a huge amount of training data, from millions of games, will contain only a tiny proportion of all possible moves. This was demonstrated very effectively when Google's DeepMind AI team used two reinforcement algorithms to play against each other. Not only did the resulting model outperform the best existing chess program at the time, but during the process the algorithm discovered completely new strategies of play, previously unknown to human grandmasters[35].

Reinforcement learning has potential, but it does have its weaknesses. One issue is that the training algorithm is bounded by the speed of the trial and error process. If a reinforcement algorithm is being trained to make mortgage lending decisions, then the time between an action being taken and assessing how successful it was could be years. Consequently, the training process will take far too long to be of practical use. DeepMind's chess playing program needed to play 68 million games to become as good as it did. It could only do this by playing against another computer, allowing games to be played in a fraction of a second[36].

OK, so being superhuman at chess is all well and good, but what are the real-world applications of reinforcement learning? I've done quite a lot of research and my conclusion is that the number of practical solutions in use today is pretty small compared to the number of supervised leaning based ones. Sure, there are lots of interesting articles about how great reinforcement learning is, but in terms of usage, the number of reinforcement learning-based solutions lags a long way behind the number of supervised learning-based ones.

One area where reinforcement learning is having an impact is in improving the efficiency of control systems in uncertain or chaotic environments. Complex systems such as power plants, heating systems and server farms have lots of controls which are adjusted to manage different parts of the system. The relationship between the controls and system performance isn't always obvious. It's not a simple case of one control impacts just one thing, everything is interconnected. Tweaking the water pressure in the cooling system to improve turbine performance has a negative impact on the efficiency of a transformer further down the line. Just like the chess problem, where there is an almost infinite number of possible games that can be played, in a power plant there are an almost infinite number of combinations of control settings. Reinforcement learning finds better ways of setting the controls through trial and error, to optimize the overall efficiency of the system. This mirrors the way an experienced engineer uses their knowledge and intuition, learnt over many years of practice, as to what the systemwide effects of tweaking different controls are likely to be.

Another area where reinforcement learning shows promise is in robotics. This is to train robots to carry out complex manual task that could previously only be undertaken by a trained person. A robotic device is given the task of doing something like pulling pints, sorting parts or stacking shelves. Through a process of trial and error they can potentially learn to do this very effectively.

4. The Impact of AI on Everyday Life

Today, AI-based technologies are improving business processes to deliver products and services more efficiently. They are also helping to advance scientific knowledge, improve our understanding of complex environmental issues and a host of other things. Governments and city authorities are also using AI to improve the quality of public services and the urban environment.

At a personal level, we're also seeing AI improving our day-to-day experiences in almost everything we do. Many of these are simple things that we're hardly aware of. Things work just a little bit better and require less effort on our part. Predictive text, controlling your car via voice command and streaming service recommendations have all benefited from the application of AI.

But what about the dark side? How are governments, corporations and other organizations using AI to decide how people are assessed, profiled, manipulated and controlled?

The powers in society have always sought to influence people in pursuit or their goals. The difference this time around is that the tools organizations are employing are much more powerful and can be targeted more accurately than ever before. This is partly due to new AI-based technologies, but equally important is the data flowing from our smart devices, social media and a variety of other sources, to the server farms controlled by those various powers.

One concern is that a lot of artificial intelligence is being deployed in an ad-hoc way such that it slips under the radar. There isn't a single shadowy super organization developing lots of nasty tech or a mad robot dictator working towards world domination. Instead, we risk losing control piecemeal to the machines one decision at a time[37]. A retailer deploys an AI tool to decide who its customers should be. A government automates some services to track criminal suspects. A hospital uses an automated assessment tool to decide who should be prioritized for treatment. You get fired because some AI selection tool assigned you to the redundancy pool and so on. Before you know it, AI-based decision-making is impacting almost everything you do. This gives those who control AI tech enormous power. The tech itself isn't deciding to pursue some overarching goal of ultimate control. It's merely a tool, used by those who control the tech, to manipulate us for their own ends.

In some countries, governments are adopting AI-powered technology to track and monitor entire populations to identify "Individuals of interest"[38] who don't conform to social norms. In principle, this is similar to credit scoring, but instead of calculating your credit score, the algorithm produces a "Social score" representing your qualities as a citizen. Score highly and the world is your oyster. You can get a promotion, open a new bank account and all the other things that one expects to be able to do in society. However, if you get a low score, then that indicates you have undesirable qualities. Your activities will be restricted, and if necessary, intervention taken to bring your behavior back in line with the accepted norm. These types of AI application are a risk to human rights, restricts freedom of expression and threatens democratic principles.

You might think this type of individual assessment would only be carried out by oppressive regimes. However, many governments around the world, including those in Europe and North America, are using similar tools to identify "Undesirables" within their populations. Large corporations, including Facebook and Uber, have also been reported to have profiled their customers and employees in a similar way[39]. Only this time, score low enough and you risk being sacked, censored or having your account closed, without being provided with a detailed explanation as to what you may have done wrong.

That's the scary bit. I'm not saying that all, or even most, uses of this type of AI-based control are necessarily wrong – far from it. When a government uses artificial intelligence for social benefit, I think that's great. If it's used to identify vulnerable people who need support or to improve education and so on, then that's a very good thing if executed appropriately[40]. It helps individuals directly, but it also frees up resources to spend on other things that society needs. Likewise, using AI to detect illegal sexist or racist material, or to restrict fake news, is a good thing if applied in the right way.

Things are also rarely clear cut. The underlying technology isn't intrinsically good or bad. It's that old adage about how it's used that determines if good or evil is dispensed. Take facial recognition. Used in the right way, it's a powerful tool to fight crime, find missing persons, speed you through customs when on holiday and whole host of other things.

A key issue with all these examples is intent. Are decisions being made for organizational gain or for the benefit of individuals and/or society? Whether the intent is for good or ill, it's when AI tech is combined with huge amounts of personal data that some of the most significant issues arise. The computers, when trained with vast amounts of detailed personal information, can anticipate our behaviors very accurately.

One way these insights are used is to reinforce our existing intentions to ensure we carry through. If there's a tendency for us to do something that an organization wants us to do, then they'll encourage us to do that. With marketing, it's all about exposing us to influences, such as ads and product placement, to tip us over the edge and buy something that we're interested in. Conversely, if our intentions are counter to what they want, then organizations will act to discourage us. Negative campaigning in politics is a prime example. Imagine I'm a right (or left) wing politician. I want to find the left (or right) wing voters inclined to vote for a certain candidate, but who can be persuaded to switch their allegiance if I stream negative media stories about that candidate to them.

The other way organizations apply their AI-driven insights is to prevent us doing things or to force us down a particular route. In government, decisions about state benefits, identifying fraudsters, deciding which prisoners to grant parole too and so on, are increasingly being made by AI-driven automated decision-making systems. If the computer says no, then that's that.

To their merit, this type of automated decision-making can drive efficiencies in government departments if deployed appropriately. This is by automatically determining the best options for benefit claimants, hospital patients, tax payers or whoever without needing to pay salaried employees to do it. However, badly designed systems disadvantage the poor and vulnerable by leaving no route against which to appeal the decisions made by the machines[41]. Unless these automated decision-making systems are understood and sufficiently transparent, then the risk of harm, intended or otherwise, is very real. It's therefore important to understand what decisions artificial intelligence is being used to make, what data is being used and what impact these decisions have upon our rights and freedoms. Perhaps most importantly, we need to understand who designs and controls these systems and understand their goals and motivations.

One of the biggest concerns about AI-driven decision-making is unjust discrimination; by which I mean *unfairly* discriminating against people with certain characteristics. Let's make no mistake, pretty much all decision-making systems, AI-based or not, work on the principle of discrimination. Returning to the scorecard of Figure 3, the scorecard favors those with high incomes, own their own homes and so on. You're disadvantaged if you rent or don't earn a lot. If you don't have discrimination then you don't have informed decision-making. You might as well follow the Dice Man's[42] example and make all your important life decisions by just rolling the die.

Another take on the issue of discrimination is not if discrimination exists, but is that discrimination something that society deems to be unfair (unethical) or illegal? i.e. biased.

It's a mistake to think that AI-based algorithms naturally create bias in decision-making. Rather, they highlight biases that existed historically. They hold up a mirror to our own human failings when deciding how to treat each other. The problem really starts with the training data that we've created, not the algorithms that learn from it. It's a little sad, but very educational, to find that as artificial intelligence becomes more widely used, so we are seeing just how biased human beings have been in the past, in almost every walk of life, to some degree or other.

Although we tend to talk about bias as a single thing, there are actually two different manifestations of bias. The first is historic *decision bias*. If we continue to think about the scorecard of Figure 3, the reason eye color features in the scorecard is because, in the past, lenders unfairly discriminated against non-white loan applicants who were more likely to have certain eye colors. When two people with identical profiles applied for credit, white people predominately got credit while non-white people tended to be declined. The training data captures the flawed lending decisions made in the past, and hence, these flaws are carried forward into the scorecard that was developed using that data.

Another well-cited example of racial bias is in parole granting decisions in the US. For years, algorithms have been widely used to decide which prisoners should be granted parole on the basis of a "Likelihood to reoffend score." Get a low score and you get your parole, but score high and you stay in jail. It has been suggested that some of these algorithms are fundamentally racist[43]. This is because they have been developed using historic data that was itself racist in nature. The algorithms didn't decide to be racist. They just turned out of that way because the training data was imperfect.

The second type of bias is *sample bias*. There's nothing wrong with individual items of data or the decisions that the data captures.

Instead, certain groups are under or over-represented. The training data may contain disproportionately too many young people, under-represent people with disabilities, have more people from one gender than another and so on.

A well-publicized example of this type of bias was seen with the role out of facial recognition software. Many facial recognition systems were developed using training data that contained pictures of predominately white men. This data may have been gathered perfectly legally, with the privacy and data protection rights of those individuals being managed ethically and within the law. However, it should have been no surprise, that when police forces started using these systems to spot suspected criminals in public places, women and people from non-white ethnic backgrounds were subject to more errors and mistakes than white men[44]. The data didn't include a diverse enough range of people to ensure a consistent level of accuracy for everyone. Consequently, they were stopped, searched and arrested more often than they should have been. Some organizations rolled out facial-recognition systems even when they knew in advance that these issues existed[45].

Bias is one problem but another issue is social exclusion. In many walks of life, there are groups of people who have become increasingly sidelined from mainstream society. Artificial intelligence isn't solely responsible for this, but it may be a contributing factor.

We may all be individually assessed by an unbiased, AI-based decision-making system, with everyone having their own unique prediction made about their behavior that's then used to make decisions about how to treat them. Therefore, if the system is unbiased, in one sense, everyone is considered fairly on their own merits. However, people with similar, "Negative", traits will always tend to end up on wrong side of the decision-making process. If you get offered a raw deal for one type of product or service, it's likely you'll get a raw deal for other things as well. The people who can't get a mortgage also tend to be those that can't get insurance, a secure job and so on.

One reason for this is the highly accurate, real-time, predictions that artificial intelligence can make about people. As AI-based decision-making becomes better, so everything becomes more precise and clear cut. Sometimes this is great. If I'm worried I've got cancer, and an AI-based diagnostic tool can determine if I have the disease faster and more accurately than a human doctor, then everyone wins. But from a societal perspective, improved accuracy isn't always a good thing.

Take insurance, for your car, house, healthcare or whatever. The whole thing works on the premise of pooled risk. Everyone pays their premium into a central pot. If someone has a mishap the pot pays out. Over time, insurers have realized that some people carry a higher risk than others. Therefore, some people pay more for their insurance. I think that that's fine to a degree, but imagine that the insurer can make near perfect predictions about people. If they predict that I have almost zero chance of making a claim but estimate that your chance of claiming is pretty much 100% What happens then?

In this scenario, having insurance becomes pointless for everyone except the insurer. The insurance company will only provide insurance to people who'll almost never claim and hence don't need insurance (me in this example). Those people that need insurance can't get it (that's you!) An extreme example maybe, but this is the direction of travel as more data about us becomes available and the AI-based decision-making tools that organizations use become increasingly accurate in predicting our behaviors[46].

Some argue that these actions are fine – they are examples of businesses becoming ever more efficient for the benefit of their shareholders[47]. Others however, argue that it creates a divide in our society. Some, perhaps most, benefit from the advances that artificial intelligence brings in terms of better products and services, targeted pricing and so on, but a growing minority are being marginalized to a greater degree than in previous generations.

Another example is dating. These days, more Americans meet

their partners online than in person[48]. But how are you introduced to prospective partners? The most popular dating sites have millions of users. You can't review everyone's profile so the computers rank everyone in terms of their compatibility. You only see the matches the computer has put at the top of its list, and it's the people behind the website who decide what constitutes a good match[49]. It might not be the case for every dating site, but most are commercial ventures. If they are ruthlessly following the profit motive, then it will be in their interest for you to continue to meet new people so that you use their service for as long as possible, rather than helping you find a long term partner – if that's what you want.

Then we come to the issue of diversity. Sure, you can choose from thousands of potential dates but there are people with certain tendencies, hobbies and behaviors, who you'll never be introduced to simply because the algorithms deem you won't make a good match. But what does that mean? Who are the algorithms keeping apart and who is being forced together? Does this approach encourage people to mix between different social, ethnic and economic groups, or does it promote segregation by ensuring that you always meet people just like you?

And it's not just dating where we see a potential loss of diversity. In theory, we now live in a world of almost endless choice. However, the same types of algorithms used in dating are also used to present us with recommendations for all sorts of other products and services[50] This ranges from the books and music we read and listen to, to the news and websites we are directed to on social media to the products we buy. The whole thing acts as a feedback loop. The more we follow the recommendations we are given, so the more of those types of recommendation are suggested to us. Consequently, your whole outlook becomes increasingly narrow.

Resistance to the unfettered applications of artificial intelligence, and to how our personal data is used, also continues to grow. In the early 2000s, tech companies could do almost whatever they wanted to with your data. Consequently, they used it to make as much money as possible with little regard of the impact it might have upon people. However, the tide is now turning. As we'll discuss in Chapter 6, many governments are increasingly thinking about the ethics of personal data and automated decision-making (based on AI technologies). Consequently, many are reacting to address the concerns that have been raised about who has access to our data and how that data is used.

5. The Changing Nature of Work

A common questions people ask is: "Am I going to lose my job to a Robot?" Maybe. There are two ways that artificial intelligence is being used in the workplace:

1. **Automation.** People are replaced by computers, robots or other machines. The people who used to do those jobs are laid off.

2. **Augmentation.** The machines provide added capability. This allows people to do their jobs better than before.

A lesson from previous technological advancements is that just because a technology is useful, or is better than what already exists, doesn't mean universal adoption is immediate or inevitable. When it comes to automation and augmentation, the questions that people should ask are:

- How much of each will occur?
- What professions will be impacted and to what degree?
- When and over what timescales?
- Where will they occur, in what countries and regions?

If our AI-driven future is all about augmentation, then that's great. We'll do everything better than before, improving outcomes for businesses, customers and ourselves. However, if most jobs are automated, then that's going to cause all sorts of problems. At a simplistic level, if no one has a job then no one can buy anything and the economy collapses. It doesn't matter that a robot can stock the shelves of your local store for a fraction of the cost of a human worker if no one can afford to buy what's on the shelves.

Automation is obviously worrying because of its potential impact on our livelihoods. Therefore, let's start by thinking about what the effects of automation might be.

If we think about the recent past, first world economies underwent huge technological upheavals in final decades of the 20th century. The near death of the loan underwriting profession, that's been a theme throughout this book, is just one of many professions that have all but disappeared due to technological advances in the last few decades. Switchboard operators, film projectionists and typesetters are just a few other examples of jobs that effectively no longer exist. Similarly, the automation of manufacturing processes across swathes of industry in the 1980s and 1990s, was a key factor in the decimation of the workforce in those industries during that time[51].

If we take a look at another major industry sector, farming, then in the middle of the 19th Century, around 22% of the UK population was employed in agriculture[52]. By the start of the 21st Century, this figure was below 1% A massive reduction driven by a mixture of evolution and revolution in farming methods. This included the introduction of ever more complex machinery to replace tasks such as sowing, reaping and threshing that were once mainstay activities of the farming process[53]. If we are talking about AI automating farming, then you could argue that it's a bit late for that – most of the jobs have already gone. Sure, artificial intelligence may reduce that 1% figure a bit more, but it's very much the icing on the cake rather than the cake itself.

The message I am trying to get across is that change and automation has been occurring for decades. Concerns over job security and the impact of technology is not new either. It's just that this time round we have a different sort of technology, AI, added into the mix. Asking if more jobs are going to be automated in the future due to AI isn't really the right question to ask – the question has only one answer – of course some jobs will be lost. This is because it's been demonstrated beyond doubt that artificial intelligence can facilitate doing many things better, quicker and cheaper than a real person can in many industries and professions. A much better questions to ask is:

Are AI technologies so different, that they will result in an unprecedented acceleration in automation and rising unemployment, the likes of which we have never seen before?

If AI is just a means of continuing current trends in automation then no problem, it's just business as usual. No point getting hot under the collar about it. Some jobs will become redundant and disappear, some will adapt and change. Others will see more people employed in those sectors, and in some areas, completely new types of job will be created.

If, on the other hand, the rate of change increases significantly because artificial intelligence brings something else to the table, then that's a concern. The important factor is the balance between job losses in one sector and the rate that new jobs are created somewhere else.

So, which way will things go? It's difficult to tell, but let's look at what some experts in the field have said and also examine some trends being seen in the economy.

A very influential study of its time, back in 2013[54], estimated that 47% of jobs in the US were at high risk of being lost due to automation by about 2035[55]. The figures for other advanced economies, such as Germany and the UK, were similar. That's pretty scary stuff, but things have mellowed somewhat since then. More recent figures from the OECD.[56] estimate that only around 14% of jobs might go. The OECD also acknowledged that this figure was only looking at job losses and didn't take into account all of the extra jobs that were expected to be created.

This seems to be where are today; i.e. no more than about 10-15% of jobs will go in the next 10 – 20 years due to AI-driven automation. Also, we are not talking about these things occurring overnight but over many years. One way to think about this is say, you work in a team of 20 people then, over the next 20 years, that may reduce to 17 or 18, all other things being equal.

It's good to consider what people are predicting will happen in the future, but let's not forget what's already happened. The past informs the future and we'd be remiss not to consider how things have been going to date. It was probably around 2010[57] when concerns about the impacts machine learning and AI first began to be voiced. So, we've got a good few years of this new technology behind us. Given all the great things we are being told this tech is being used to automate, from driverless vehicles to fully automated warehouses to robotic customer service reps, I'd expect to be seeing their impact on the economy by now.

One very obvious thing to look at is unemployment rates. These should be rising – surely? Figure 9 shows the pattern of unemployment in the US[58] over the fifty-year period between 1970 and the start of 2020[59].

In Figure 9, the troughs correlate with recessions and the peaks with the boom times. You can clearly see the rise in unemployment during the recession following the dot.com bubble of the early 2000s and the fallout from the sub-prime mortgage crisis later that decade. Figure 9 doesn't show much that supports rising unemployment. If anything, it shows the converse. The fall in unemployment between 2010 and 2020 was greater than at any time in recent history.

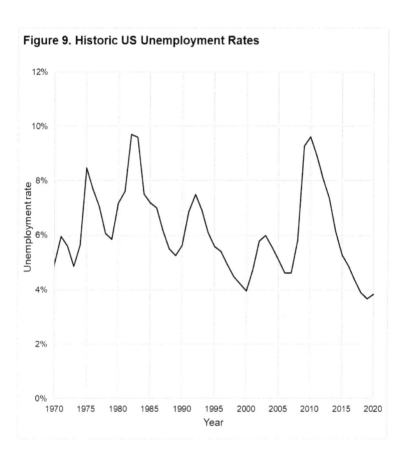

Figure 9. Historic US Unemployment Rates

Now, you've got to be extremely careful about drawing conclusions from a single data series like this. However, to date, there doesn't seem to have been a noticeable effect on overall employment levels in the US due to AI. If you look at trends in other employment related metrics, such as average wages or productivity[60] then, over recent years, there also seems to be very little outside of the normal rise and fall that follows economic cycles. There is no evidence of the step change in productivity or rising unemployment that many have talked about. Maybe that will change in future, and some have argued that the 2020 covid-19 pandemic could accelerate the use of AI-driven automation[61], but as it stands, there isn't much evidence of a new wave of robot takeovers in the workplace yet.

Why is this the case? Maybe AI is leading to new forms of employment. It's not just a case of technicians identifying a business process done by people and replacing it with a robot. Employers are taking advantage of the extra resources that automation frees up to do other things[62].

Another possibility is that companies are engaged in the Red Queen's Race[63]. You have to invest and improve just to keep up. A few years ago, all I needed to succeed as an on-line retailer was a nice website, but now, I need to build real-time individually tailored customer interaction into my site, apply sentiment analysis to assess what people think about it and build chatbots to keep customers engaged. My internet marketing team isn't dispensed with, they are just refocused on the next set of tasks in the never-ending race against my rivals. If anything, maybe I need even more people just to keep on top of everything.

A different perspective is that while almost all medium to large organizations are talking-up the benefits of AI-driven automation, few have really understood how to apply AI effectively. They haven't been able to fully integrate AI into their business processes and strategically realign their organizations to reap the benefits that these new technologies offer.

A considerable proportion of AI projects have failed or delivered less than expected because organizations have not approached things in the right way. Several studies have put the failure rate for business AI projects at well over 50% with the most pessimistic estimating that almost 9 out of 10 business have seen their AI initiatives fail to fully deliver[64].

An easy mistake to make is to hire a load of those mysterious data scientist types without really understanding what you want them for. The data scientists turn up at the office, with more PhDs than you can count, and then apply their technical wizardry to problems and processes that they have no real understanding of. Just like any other technology, artificial intelligence must be shaped to fit what an organization does. This needs to include all of the soft issues involving people, the law, social customs, customer service and reputational impact. Technology on its own isn't enough.

There may be not a huge amount of evidence for rising unemployment or other impacts at a national level – yet, but some professions are more at risk than others. Artificial intelligence is most effective at supporting the automation of tasks when:

- Tasks are well defined. You can understand clearly what's involved in doing it.

- There's lots of data about the task for the AI to learn from.

- There are clear decisions or outcomes that are required, based on the data available for training.

- The tasks are frequent and repeatable.

- A task is measurable. It's easy to determine if the task was performed well, or not.

When it comes to the low hanging fruit, if you work in an industry where lots of people are doing lots of similar things, or making certain types of decision on a frequent basis, then these are the roles most at risk. Even if the task you do is very complex or requires a lot of training, that doesn't reduce your vulnerability. If what you do is something that can be distilled down to a set of clear-cut actions, decisions and outcomes, then your job is at risk.

The more diverse and one-off the type of work, and the broader the span of someone's responsibilities, the harder it is to develop an AI-based tool to perform that role effectively. That's not to say that an AI won't be developed that can do that role at some point in the future but that it's not feasible or cost effective to replace you yet.

There are also some jobs where only a person will do because, it's argued, we value human interaction over the ruthless efficiency of a machine. Personally, I like being served in my local pub by a real person. I don't want a machine pulling my pint for me.

In education, the 1:1 experience is also hard to replace. There are educational robots around that can interact with students to support their education, by asking and answering questions, but they are very crude devices compared to a typical human teacher.

However, many people take the opposite view. For many mundane tasks, like checking you bank balance or buying a loaf of bread, then having a machine take your money is actually preferred. This is precisely because you don't have to waste effort interacting with some stranger who you may never meet again.

If you take all that together, then it's things like manufacturing and warehousing, transportation, retail services (such as call centers) and back office functions (routine admin/paperwork) where jobs are most likely to be affected. This is because they involve following a certain set of frequently repeated procedures and behaviors that can be learnt by a computer and/or acted upon by a robot. Professional and personal services, education, healthcare and the arts are areas where jobs are less prone to robot takeover[65] - although that's not to say that many functions that support these roles can't be automated.

Massive job losses due to AI-driven automation is something that many people fear. However, the other side of the coin is augmentation. Maybe no one needs to lose their job, but the job you do can be done so much more effectively if AI is deployed to help you. Your job won't disappear, but you are going to need to adapt to doing a different set of tasks in a different way. You'll need to accept that new technology is going to do some of the heavy lifting for you, to free up your time to do all the other, more important things, that you never spent enough time on before.

The aforementioned study by the OECD concluded that only about 14% of jobs will be automated in the next few years. However, it also said that nearly half of jobs in developed countries would be impacted by AI in some way, requiring retraining and/or reorientation.

How will AI-driven augmentation help you in your work? Well, a lot of it covers the same principles as automation. It's about having a machine doing things that you might have done before, but quicker and better. However, we are in augmentation territory when two conditions exist:

1. There are a number of important, significant or time-consuming tasks that the machines can't do very well, or do as effectively as a person.

2. There are lots of extra things that you could be doing, if you had the time. Having some AI-powered assistance will allow you to do those things.

Law is one profession already seeing the benefits of AI-driven augmentation. The law in its entirety covers a huge span of activities and variety of cases. This ranges from high profile murder cases, to mass market claims for road accidents, divorce and home insurance. The media have reported cases of "Robot judges" dispensing justice, and maybe that will one day be the norm, but the areas of law that are currently being impacted most by AI include:

- **Collating documents.** AI technologies, such as document clustering, can reduce the time spent trawling through the mass of case law to find all the relevant legal documents that might support a case.

- **Conviction prediction.** Given information about a case, what's the chance that the accused will be convicted? A defence lawyer might push for a plea bargain rather than acquittal if their AI helper concludes that the odds are against them.

- **Triage**. AI is used to gauge how difficult a case will be to resolve. A simple damages case gets handed to the office junior, whereas the most complex cases are assigned to a senior partner.

- **Claims and damages.** Based on the features of an insurance claim, divorce case etc., tools can be developed to estimate what the value of any claim/settlement should be.

Let's now consider something like education. If you can automate 20% of a teacher's job, does that mean that you can make 20% of teachers redundant? No. Why not? One reason is that in most schools leaving a classroom unattended is frowned upon. You can't just leave kids alone with a robot all day. Sure, there are some educational robots around, but these are nowhere near advanced enough to substitute for a real person. Instead, the sorts of tools that are being trialed or are on the horizon are things like:

- **Automatic registration.** Facial recognition scans the class to identify everyone whose there. The teacher only needs to confirm the status of those the system reports as absent.

- **Providing information**. Chatbots can answer a lot of the questions that parents and students have, without having to bother the teacher.

- **Student support**. Predictive models, that use student information as inputs, can predict which students might struggle with certain ideas and concepts. Teachers can then address student weaknesses *before* they become apparent.

For the private sector, it's very much about stripping out cost to boost the bottom line as much as possible, which makes automation one of the first thing that comes to mind. However, for many government departments, charities and other not-for-profit organizations, there's a different perspective. Improving efficiency is important but not to improve the bottom line. Rather, it's to deliver as much as possible. In healthcare, the demand for services is almost limitless. No amount of money can provide everyone with the very best medical care. If an artificial intelligence-based tool can diagnose and treat patients more quickly then you get doctors to treat more patients. You don't reduce the number of doctors. The same principle applies to law enforcement, education and many other public services.

The early AI evangelists were perhaps running before they could walk. They projected current trends into their ideas of the future in simplistic ways. There may come a day when a robot can do pretty much anything we can, but that day is probably many decades away. There are still many technological, legal and cultural hurdles to overcome.

For most (but not all) of us that means that our jobs are probably safe from robot takeover for the time being, with one caveat. Be prepared for change. You must be willing to adapt and accept that there will be an increasing number of AI-based tools that can enhance what you do, so that you can do your job more effectively and more efficiently than you did before.

6. Ethical AI?

Should we grant an artificial intelligence the same legal status as a person? Do robots have "Human rights?" These types of questions get a lot of media attention but we are a very long way from sentient machines who can really think for themselves. Consequently, robot rights aren't something we need to address right now and probably not for many years.

Instead, the immediate concerns about AI relate to how it's being used to monitor, influence, manipulate and control us. When talking about the ethics of AI, what we are really discussing is what constitutes ethical use by those who control it, rather than the ethics of AI itself.

Ethics isn't singular, objective or absolute. There are many different perspectives and no two people will adopt exactly the same moral stance in every situation. This is one reason why there is so much argument about the rights and wrongs of how AI-based technologies are deployed.

In coming to an ethical position about something, a key question is, do you tend to approach things from a consequentialist or non-consequentialist perspective? If you believe that anything goes if you get a good outcome, then that's a consequentialist perspective. The ends justify the means. However, if following your principles is more important, that's a non-consequentialist way of looking at things. It's as much about your journey as the final destination.

There are several forms of consequentialism, but Utilitarianism is the most well-known. Utilitarians tend to think in terms of:

"The greatest good for the greatest number."[66]

An ethical action maximizes happiness and pleasure within the population. For a utilitarian, an action is only unethical if it leads to pain or unhappiness.

To be practical, utilitarianism needs to be able to measure how much happiness and pleasure are created so that different options can be compared. In practice, this means everything gets assigned a monetary value. The outcome yielding the greatest value is deemed to be best. You can see utilitarianism in action whenever politicians talk about the "Cost/benefit" case for where to build a new hospital, airport or whatever. The upsides and downsides of each location are assigned a dollar value. Everything is added up and the option with the greatest net benefit is chosen.

Not everyone takes a consequentialist view. The philosopher Immanuel Kant argued that instead of asking what the impact of an action will be on someone, an action is ethical if it shows respect for others.

A fundamental principle of Kant's thinking is universality[67]. Ethical behavior is something all rational people agree with. Imagine that a few of us are working late in the office one night. To keep us motivated, our boss orders in a nice big pizza for us to share. Everyone might want the entire pizza for themselves but the only sensible (ethical) decision that any rational person can arrive at is to share the pizza equally amongst everyone.

Complementary to the principle of universality, Kant proposed another view of ethical behavior as one where everyone should be treated as a sentient being with the right to their own life and opinions. People should not be objectified. They aren't just a resource to use for your own ends. This is often expressed as the "Golden Rule:"

> "Do to others as you would have done to you."

The problem with the golden rule is it implies we should do stuff like giving all our money to random strangers because this is what we'd want them to do for us. Consequently, it's the inverse of the Golden Rule that's most practical: "Don't do to others as we would not have done to us." Or more simply: "Do no evil."

Another non-consequentialist framework is based on human rights. There are things we are all entitled to and certain things we can't be denied. These rights are beyond governments, states and corporations to grant or deny. Originating with the right to life, liberty and property, the concept of human rights has grown to cover a great many freedoms that we now take for granted[68].

In life, people naturally adopt ethical positions that encompass both consequentialist and non-consequentialist perspectives. They then draw their own conclusions as to what constitutes good behavior. However, what can be said to apply across all ethical frameworks, is that:

- Ethics carries with it the idea of something more important than the individual.

- An ethical action is one that the perpetrator can defend in terms of more than self-interest.

- To act ethically one must, at the very least, consider the impact of one's actions on others[69].

Let's now bring things back to the ethics of AI-driven tools that are applied to people. As I see it, there are four key aspects to consider.

1. **Personal Data.** This is all sorts of stuff such as our income, age, location data, medical records, blog posts and so on.

2. **Purpose.** What reason does someone have for using our data? Are they targeting us with adverts?, declining people for credit?, identifying you as a potential criminal? or whatever.

3. **Intent (Beneficiary).** Who gains from using your data? Is it to help you or for someone else's benefit? For example, is your health app intended to make you money or reduce my chance of getting ill?

4. **Mechanism.** How is data used to achieve the desired purpose? One aspect of this is about who makes the decisions. Is it a human or an automated AI-driven decision-making system? The other, arguably more important, aspect is understanding the underlying logic used to arrive at a decision, regardless of who makes it.

How we deal with peoples' data is invariably linked to how artificial intelligence is used and how powerful it can become. AI only operates effectively when it has large volumes of data to work with. This includes data resources (training data) to build intelligent tools in the first place but also the data required to deploy them. The credit scoring model in Figure 3 can't generate an accurate credit score for someone if you don't know what that person's income, eye color, employment status and so on are. We can exert a lot of control over how AI is developed and deployed by controlling the data it needs to function. Restrict the data artificial intelligence has access to and you reduce its ability to anticipate your behaviors, and therefore, the degree to which it can be used to control you.

In terms of purpose and intent, we have to remember that current AI only does exactly what it has been tasked to do. Misspecify the task and it won't do what you really want. Purpose is often driven by the intent of the developer. They want the AI to achieve something they've defined. If the primary intent is to generate profits, then that may drive a very different view of purpose than if the intent is to save lives, even if the app under development is being described in exactly the same way in terms of what it's meant to do.

Profit objectives and individual benefit aren't mutually exclusive, but there's a pretty torrid history of large corporations chasing the profit motive at the expense of individuals. Examples range from the tobacco industry, to the VW emissions scandal, Cambridge Analytica and pharmaceutical cover-ups to climate change denial in the fossil fuel industry. The list goes on and on. Even if the intent is altruistic in nature, if the right purpose isn't used in training the model that underpins an AI application, then that could lead to some very poor, if unintended, outcomes for people.

Finally, there is the question around mechanism. Regardless of the data, purpose and intent, how are decisions about people being made? What checks and controls are in place to ensure that the decision-making mechanism is acting in a legal, fair and ethical way?

Personal data tends to get most of the press, so let's continue to think a bit more about personal data and data protection.

As described earlier in the book, machine learning-based AI, which covers nearly all practical AI systems in use today, inherently discriminates. That's how it works. It looks for differences between things to identify what features of the environment are correlated with different outcomes. So, what data is it OK to use about people? Consider Figure 10.

Figure 10. Whose data is it anyway?

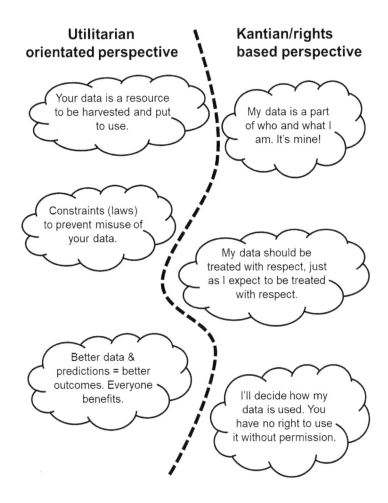

From a utilitarian perspective it's easy to argue that it's OK to use any data at all if, on balance, it results in good outcomes. From this viewpoint, data is a resource to be mined and harvested. If we can hoover up all that great data about people and use it for productive purposes, then that's fine, as long as overall society gets some net benefit. Letting Google, Apple, Amazon etc., have access to everyone's data is a good thing if they use it to develop better diagnostic tools for doctors, improve educational outcomes and so on. If the benefits justify it then it's a no brainer. If a few people are hurt or disadvantaged as a result, then that's a price worth paying. If, for any reason, using that data causes problems that we feel must be addressed, such as protecting people's medical data, then we'll draft some specific laws to deal with that particular problem.

From a rights-based perspective things look very different. The starting point is that my data is mine and your data is yours. We own it. It's a violation of our rights for someone to gather or use our data without our permission. This is regardless of whether or not you or they will benefit (or be disadvantaged) from using it. In principle, it's no different to a violation of our person or property. If someone "Borrowed" your car without asking you first, because it meant that they got some benefit from using it, that's not right, even if it didn't disadvantage you in any way.

These differences, between utilitarian and rights-based approaches, are clearly visible in the different paths that US and EU authorities have followed when it comes to data protection law.

In the US, things have been driven very much from the utilitarian camp in a piecemeal way. When there is sufficient concern over a specific way that data is being used, a law is passed to address that concern. One of the first US data laws was the 1974 Equal Credit Opportunity Act (ECOA)[70] that determines the type of data that can be used in credit granting decisions. Likewise, when concerns were raised over how private medical providers were using their patients' data, The Health Insurance Portability and Accountability Act 1996 (HIPAA) was enacted to address these concerns. There are a host of other similar laws at both state and federal level dealing with different data issues.

In Europe, the approach has been very different. Since introducing the first international data protection laws back in 1981[71], and more recently with the General Data Protection Regulation (GDPR) in 2018, it's been all about individual rights. In particular, the GDPR provides individuals with comprehensive rights over how their data is gathered and stored, and the uses to which it's put. For example, using data about peoples' race, political views and medical history is explicitly forbidden in the GDPR, unless certain specific conditions have been met[72].

The GDPR is also principle based. It's very much about the spirit of the law and doing the right thing. Consequently, very little in the GDPR is industry specific. It's very much a general approach that's intended to operate across every government and industry sector. Being principle-based means that the GDPR doesn't tell organizations exactly what they must do to comply with it. The idea is to get them to think about their responsibilities to the people they hold data about and to encourage them to act in a responsible way, rather than blindly following a rigid set of regulations. No law is perfect. However, the GDPR is a big step forward in protecting how people's data is gathered and used.

These different perspectives are one reason why many US based companies have, in the past, struggled to find common ground with EU regulators over how personal data can be gathered and used in the EU.

Looking forward, the general trend appears to be more towards the EU view. US state and federal legislation are increasingly incorporating greater elements of the data rights of people[73]. However, there is still a long way to go before US data protection laws provide the same protections as those found in the EU.

Let's now move on to think about some of issues that arise when organizations use all that data to decide how people are treated using AI-based decision-making tools; i.e. item 4 in the aforementioned list. In talking about decision-making, two (linked) subjects that often come to the fore are those of bias and explicability.

At one time, it was widely believed (somewhat naively) that because training algorithms could find the optimal way to interpret the training data, the resulting model could not show any bias. In one sense that's true. A training algorithm doesn't start with any preconceptions and doesn't display any deliberate bias. It just blindly considers the available data and learns from that. Unfortunately, what is increasingly evident, is that our past human-made decisions were often sub-optimal and biased in all sorts of ways. Consequently, the training data used to construct the models used in many AI-based systems is fundamentally flawed.

If we think back to the scorecard model in Figure 3, then the most obvious concern is the use of eye color because it's a proxy for ethnicity. The data scientist responsible for running the training algorithm should have flagged it as a concern at the outset and considered excluding it from the data used to create the model.

We obviously need to be careful about using certain types of sensitive data about people, including their race, gender, religion, sexual orientation and so on, but that's not to say this type of data shouldn't be used in some situations. There is certainly a case that if the purpose is altruistic in intent, undertaken for the benefit of the individual in question and without detriment to others, then allowing decision-making processes to use that data is ethical in some circumstances.

Certainly, in medicine, things like gender and race are correlated with certain medical conditions. On that basis, it would seem sensible to encourage people to allow this type of data to be used to help diagnose them. Another example of altruistic purpose is identifying people who don't claim all the state aid/benefits they are entitled too. This is so that you can contact them and tell them about the extra help they can get. However, using sensitive personal data to set insurance premiums, where the primary beneficiary is the insurer, or to exclude people from receiving benefits are more questionable activities.

To be able to understand and deal with bias, data is key, but we also need to be able to pick apart how decisions are arrived at using that data. We need to understand the mechanism for decision-making so that in turn we can identify where and how bias is occurring.

If we talk to a human expert about how they come to a decision, then they can usually say "Well, we think this patient has cancer because of this dark patch on the scan", or "We are going to arrest this suspect because we've got this piece of evidence that suggests we should haul them in for questioning." However, when it comes to algorithms things are often less clear.

Many algorithms, and in particular ones based on neural networks, are increasingly **black box** in nature. Black box means that you can determine what data provides the inputs to an algorithm and what outputs (decisions) come out, but you can't easily work out how all that data was combined together to deliver one decision and not another. You can see this just by looking at the differences between the scorecard and neural network versions of the credit scoring models we've considered in previous chapters (Figure 3 Vs. 6 & 7). With the scorecard, you can easily see what contributes to the final score and by how much but for the network it's not clear at all.

A lot of research is being undertaken to understanding how (deep) neural networks generate their outputs from a given set of inputs, but it's still very much an evolving element of AI-based-decision-making. A lot of progress has been made, but there's still more to do before we have a set of standardized tools that automatically explain how AI generates the outcomes and decisions that it does.

Understanding why a model produces certain outcomes doesn't solve the bias problem, but it certainly helps understand what features contribute to the decision and in what way. The GDPR also helps out EU citizens here. In particular, it requires that decisions about people should be made in a fair and transparent way[74]. People also have a right to an explanation as to how a decision was made about them[75].

In the UK, the regulator (The Information Commissioner) has drawn up a set of detailed guidelines on explicability. These indicate that a very high degree of explanation needs to be provided in terms that normal people can comprehend[76]. If someone is using a huge neural network to decide if you can get a mortgage or not, then they will need to be able to dig into that neural network and unpick how it's making its decisions. They must then explain that to you in a way that you can understand.

The UK Information Commissioner has also made it clear that if an organization doesn't have the time or money to build explicability into its product development cycle, then it should seriously consider if it should be using that technology at all. Otherwise, if it fails to provide adequate explanations to its customers, it could face fines of up to four percent of its global turnover.

Explicability is central to us being able to trust AI-based decision-making. It also supports the identification of unfair discrimination and bias in the way automated AI-based tools treat people. By laying the groundwork now, forcing developers to explain how their AI tools work, provides a key foundation for protecting us in the future as artificial intelligence becomes ever more advanced and further integrated into our daily lives. Isaac Asimov may have famously proposed his "Three laws of robotics"[77], that were designed to protect us against robot takeover, but if I were to define three laws for artificial intelligence today, then I would have explicability of action as one of them; that is: "Why did you do that robot?"

7. What Next?

Even the best futurologists frequently get it wrong when predicting which technologies will succeed, and of those technologies that do make it, most are overhyped initially even if they end up being really useful eventually[78].

A great example of this overhyping can be seen in the history of autonomous vehicles. For years, promises were made about them being publicly available within the next year or so but each year the dates were pushed back[79]. If I took my blind grandma to a typical car showroom today, I don't think I'd find anyone who'd sell her a car that then drives her home alone from the forecourt.

What it looks like now, is rather than the promise of owning a truly self-driving car that won't require a driving license to use, the near-term reality is self-driving taxis. These operate in well-defined "Geo-fenced" areas of a few major cities, overseen by human operators at taxi central. A self-driving car today doesn't mean owning something that can whisk you across states on vacation. Sure, we are going to get there one day, but it's not a universal reality yet and is unlikely to be for many years.

Perhaps the most important thing to appreciate is that technology doesn't operate in isolation. Society, law, business practices, human behavior and our fears and prejudices all have a part to play. A key reason why we don't have more driverless vehicles on the roads is that in the early days of their development not enough consideration was given to people issues. "If only we didn't have pedestrians and human drivers to worry about!" But, if anyone had given it any thought, they should have realized, right at the outset, what the problems were. The developers of self-driving cars now accept that they have to deal with these issues but it took some of them a while to get there.

It's easy for the tech sector to blame the politicians, and social and legal constraints, as the reasons why their technologies don't become more widely adopted more quickly. But the same principles apply as for any other type of invention. AI tech doesn't have an opt-out to the normal rules of engagement. If I create a super new type of cellphone, then I need to ensure it conforms with health and safety legislation so that I don't fry consumers' brains. If I develop a great tasting new food additive, then let's get that fully tested before putting it in baby food and so on.

I don't complain that the law is an ass when it comes to these areas. I make sure I understand what regulations apply and what I need to do to comply before rushing ahead with mass producing my product. In fact, I should be talking about these things in the very first design meeting. Delivering a commercial product to the market is very much the last link in the chain.

The tech sector is learning but we can still see evidence of this narrow "Tech first" thinking in practice. For example, with the "Move fast and break things" philosophy popular with some Silicon Valley entrepreneurs[80]. Get the technology working and out to market as quickly as you can, and then worry about any problems later. Take crypto-currencies such as Bitcoin and the Facebook backed Libra. Their inventors clearly didn't give enough consideration to the role and function of the regulatory authorities[81]. The barriers to their wider use, and the reason why you can't pay your taxes with them[82], have nothing to do with the underlying "Blockchain" technology that many crypto-currencies are based upon. The biggest challenge is satisfying central banks and regulatory authorities that they won't undermine the stability of the world's financial systems. Financial regulators have huge powers. They will only allow a new currency to become legal tender once all risks have been understood and mitigated against.

Without an appreciation of the context in which a technology is being applied it's easy to fall into the trap of thinking that just because it's technologically possible it will happen. The fact that someone can build an intelligent fridge, that knows when you are running out of milk and reorders it for you automatically, doesn't mean that customers want that feature in a fridge. Or maybe they do, but not because they'll ever use it to buy milk, but because they can tell all their friends and neighbors about it. It's a status symbol rather than something practically useful. Goodness knows the number of drivers who bought cars with self-park features who, after showing them off once, never used them again, or the mountains of VR headsets that now lie idle.

As you may gather, my view is that the technology is often the easy part. People are far more difficult to deal with. I'm not saying AI tech isn't enormously complex, and it only exists because of some very clever people, but the fundamental elements of AI systems are a lot easier to get to grips with than the nuances of the human condition. This makes it difficult to make accurate predictions about the future of specific AI technologies. However, barring the zombie apocalypse or complete climate collapse, then over the next five to ten years, the things I'd be willing to put my money on are:

1. Existing artificial intelligence is only going to get better. It'll become ever more prevalent in industry, our homes, schools, hospitals, and almost everywhere else.

2. We won't see the development of a self-aware, conscious Super AI with general intelligence, that is equal or better than our own, using current technologies (apology or sigh of relief as appropriate).

It can be easy to write-off some AI technologies due the flaws they exhibited when they were first put into commercial use, but many applications of artificial intelligence are still at a relatively early stage of their development. They will improve and get better in time and existing weaknesses will be addressed. In Chapter 1, I made quite a big deal about all those flawed object recognition systems, you remember, the ones that couldn't recognize an upside-down bus and so on? Well, I don't expect it will be long before that problem is solved.

Many other issues with existing artificial intelligence applications, such as the gender bias that resulted in Amazon decommissioning its hiring AI[83] or the issues over racial bias seen in some facial recognition systems, are solvable problems. This is because the issues are mainly to do with the training data used to create the models, rather than the underlying technology itself. Get the training data right and the bias disappears. As these problems are solved, we'll see ever more examples of this type of AI being deployed. Conceivably, in almost any area where decision-making capability is required and there is sufficient good quality data available to feed the training algorithms with.

Finally, what about the prospect of developing a fully artificial thinking entity any time soon? A conscious, thinking, Super AI with greater capacity to learn and reason than any human?

The first question to ask is, is such a thing even possible? Let's start by proposing that the human brain is nothing more than a very complex biological machine that conforms to the laws of nature. If that's true, then I can't think of any theoretical barrier to engineering something that's at least as good as what blind evolution can come up with, even if we don't know how to do that today. However, if you believe that there is some spirit form, a soul or something else required for conscious intelligence, then maybe we'll never get there unless we find a way to create that "Essence of intelligence" in one form or another.

Assuming that the brain does conform to the laws of nature,

then in terms of when we'll get to general AI, then that's a difficult call. However, I don't think that we'll get there using current approaches, even if we can scale up the computer power available by several orders of magnitude.

I don't disagree that practical applications of artificial intelligence have grown at a fantastic rate, and this has resulted in many sophisticated applications with capabilities that were almost unimaginable just a few years ago. If you project these advances forward in a simplistic way, then it may seem that it can't be many years before the machines can outthink us in all significant ways. However, nearly all of these recent advances in artificial intelligence have been based on variants of a single approach; that is, applying massive computational power to artificial neural networks in one form or another.

Almost everyone working in artificial intelligence is focused on neural network-based approaches. Only very small amounts of research effort are looking at alternatives. This means we could end up missing something important in the search for full AI because not enough people are looking the problem more broadly. I'm not saying that neural networks aren't immensely important to the development of AI but, if we only consider neural networks, then we're probably missing something vitally important for developing AI further.

What we are seeing is that the applications resulting from neural network approaches are increasingly powerful when it comes to singular problem-solving tasks (Narrow AI), but we don't yet seem to be near the point where we have tools that go much beyond that. The best we have today is the idea of sticking a lot of very good narrow AI together, and then adding in some human expertise to define additional rules and over-rides. This delivers something slightly "Fatter" than a single application can provide on its own, but falls short of the dream of general AI.

Another thing that worries me about current neural network approaches is how inefficient they are. It takes hundreds of high-end computers, burning millions of kilowatts of electricity, to build an advanced AI app that does just one thing very well. A well-documented example, that illustrates this issue very well, is with object recognition systems. Show a young child a single picture of a puppy once, and they'll pretty much be able to identify any dog they see. However, an object recognition system needs to be trained with thousands of images to be as good as that.

This makes me think that we aren't doing something quite right. Or, maybe we're missing something. A simple organic human brain can learn to do thousands of things pretty well (if not quite as well as a computer) using only about 20 watts of power and a lump of organic matter, weighing on average, only about 1,400 grams. Admittedly, it takes us years to learn all these things, but we still have learning capabilities that the machines can't yet match. In particular, some of the biggest research challenges relate to comprehension and understanding that allows us to exhibit common sense. To take learning from the wider world and pull out things that are relevant to a completely different set of problems. We can contextualize ideas and tasks within a broader understanding of the world and how it operates. This is both in physical terms about how things interact with each other, but equally, intellectual concepts such as ethics, religion, society and politics.

This leads me to fall into the camp that believes that there's some essence of consciousness intelligence that we've not discovered or understood yet. No amount of raw computing power is going to be enough to generate full artificial intelligence. I'm not saying that this is a soul or spirit, but there are more scientific discoveries that need to be made before we really understand consciousness, what it means to be self-aware and what human intelligence actually is. Until those breakthroughs occur, I expect we'll continue to see more developments in terms of an ever-increasing number of clever AI-based apps and robots for certain tasks, but we won't see a human equivalent (or better) general thinking machine. If those discoveries are made this year, then it may not be very long before such a machine is built. If, on the other hand, it takes decades more research, then it will be quite a long time before we cede world dominance to the computers.

As a final note, if we ever do develop artificial intelligence that's comparable or superior to human intelligence then it probably won't be in the form of human-like robots. Instead, it's likely to be a centralized entity. By that, I mean one or more of these intelligences will be housed in server farms somewhere. They won't be physically present where we can see them. In that way, size and energy requirements are almost unimportant. If the AI needs a giant computer complex, the size of a mountain in California or Beijing, then that's fine. It can then communicate and control devices around the world via the internet. It may interact with us via a robot body but the AI itself could be thousands of miles away.

Appendix A. Further Reading

If you find artificial intelligence interesting and want to know more, then the following are some other publications that may be of interest. All are non-technical in nature; i.e. no complex math or formulas.

Paul Daugherty and James Wilson. (2018). *Human + Machine: Reimaging Work in the Age of AI.* **Harvard Business Press.** This book presents a nicely optimistic view of a future in which artificial intelligence supports humans in the workplace rather than supplanting them.

Hannah Fry. (2019). *Hello World: How to be Human in the Age of the Machine.* **Black Swan.** A well-written, non-technical introduction to the world of algorithms, machine learning and artificial intelligence. Probably the book I would recommend first to someone wanting an easy-going entrée to the subject (apart from this book of course!)

Cate O'Neil. (2016). *Weapons of Math Destruction. How Big Data Increases Inequality and Threatens Democracy.* **Allen Lane.** While many authors talk about all the upsides, O'Neil presents the dark underbelly of automated decision-making. In particular, she discusses the bias and discrimination that can be brought to bear through the use and misuse of automated decision-making systems. This book is a great accompaniment to "The Age of Surveillance Capitalism" by Shoshan Zuboff.

Stuart Russell. (2019). *Human Compatible: AI and the Problem of Control.* **Allen Lane.** This book looks ahead to consider the problems we might face should we ever build super-human intelligences and how we might go about protecting ourselves against them. A good compliment to Max Tegmark's book on the possible future of AI (See below).

New Scientist. https://www.newscientist.com/ If you want a weekly digest of all that is going on in the world of science and technology, presented in an intelligent but non-technical way, then there are few publications better than this. You can pretty much guarantee that there will be at least one article on developments in AI and machine learning every week.

Max Tegmark. (2017). *Life 3.0: Being Human in the Age of Artificial Intelligence.* **Penguin.** A provocative look into the potential, risks and dangers of artificial intelligence and its relationship to humanity now and what might eventually come to pass in the future.

Shoshan Zuboff. (2019). *The Age of Surveillance Capitalism: The Fight for a Human Future at the New Frontier of Power.* **Public Affairs.** This book really digs into the issue of privacy and control, and how organizations have used their unfettered access to our personal data to boost their bottom lines at our expense.

Appendix B. Glossary

The following are explanations of common terms used in artificial intelligence and machine learning.

Accuracy. Accuracy is a measure of how often decision-making systems get things right. It is calculated as the proportion of times the system makes a correct decision. If an object recognition system is shown 50 pictures and correctly identifies 48 of them, then it's 96% accurate (100% * 48 / 50).

Activation function. This is an equation that forms one part of an artificial neuron. The main purpose of the activation function is to force a neuron's output to lie within a fixed range so that all of the neurons in a neural network produce values that have the same scale. Most commonly, the activation function forces the output to be in the range 0 and 1. Popular activation functions are the "Logistic function" and the "Hyperbolic tangent function."

Algorithm. A set of instructions, executed one after another, to complete a given task. In the world of AI, algorithms can broadly be split into two types. Training algorithms are used to discover patterns in data and to create the models the drive most AI applications. Once a model has been created, the model is itself implemented as an algorithm; i.e. the steps required process data through the model and to act upon the output(s) produced.

Android. An intelligent robot with human-like appearance that behaves in a human-like way.

Artificial Intelligence (AI). There isn't a single universally accepted definition of what AI is. However, a reasonable working definition is: The replication of biological analytical and decision-making capabilities. Examples of AI include: digital personal assistants that can answer questions, identifying what an object is in an image, vetting job applicants and the ability to beat human players at games such as chess, poker and Go.

Big Data. Any large and varied collection of data. The term is usually used to describe data sets that are too large and complex to be processed easily using a standard laptop/PC. Big Data technologies make use of advanced computer architectures and specialist software to facilitate the rapid processing of these data sets, often in real time. AI/Machine learning is one of the primary tools used to extract value from Big Data.

Black box. A system is considered to be black box in nature if it's difficult to determine how the inputs into the system relate to the outputs generated. Systems that utilize complex neural network and/or ensemble models are often described as being black box, whereas simple scorecard, decision tree and rule-based systems are not.

Byte. The basic unit of data storage for computer systems. This sentence contains about 50 bytes of data. A photo typically requires several million bytes (several megabytes) of storage and a full HD movie several billion (Several gigabytes). See also, Terabyte and Petabyte.

Causation. The reason why something happened. For example, if asking the question: "Why do plants grow more in the summer than in the winter" two facts are presented. (1) It's warmer in the summer. (2) people take more holiday in the summer. Plant growth is correlated with people taking more holiday, but not caused by it. However, plant growth is both correlated with and caused by warmer weather.

Chatbot. An app that can interact with someone in a human-like way via speech or text. Typically, a chatbot that you are likely to encounter today, is designed to provide answers to questions about a specific topic. For example, an insurer's chatbot might answer questions about the company's insurance products via their website. Most chatbots are relatively basic and are used to automate simple, frequently asked, questions in order to improve call center efficiency. More complex or unusual questions are referred to human staff to answer.

Classification model. A predictive model that estimates the probabilities of different outcomes (events). For example, based on the pattern of pixels in an image, there is a 95% probability that the thing in the image is a cat, 4% that it's a dog and 1% that it's a fish. The prediction made by the model is that the image contains a cat, because that has the highest probability associated with it. Another example is a credit scoring model. The model predicts the probability of a customer defaulting on their loan. See also, regression model.

Classification and Regression Tree (CART), *See* decision tree.

Cluster(ing). Clusters are groups that contain people or things with similar traits. For example, people with similar ages and incomes might be in one cluster, those with similar job roles and family sizes in another. Clustering algorithms are a form of unsupervised learning (see below).

Convoluted (neural) network. A deep neural network where not all neurons in one layer are connected to all the neurons in the next layer. With fewer weights, the very considerable time required to train a network is much reduced. A classic application is object recognition. Imagine you have an image comprising 256 * 256 (65,536) pixels. A traditional neural network would need 65,536 weights for each neuron in the first layer, one for each pixel. By segmenting the image into say, 64 sub-regions each with 32 *32 pixels and only connecting neurons within each sub-region, the number of weights is reduced to just 1,024 per neuron. This works because the most important features in images are usually close together (i.e. in the same or neighboring sub-regions). Pixels at opposite sides of the image are much less important.

Correlation. One variable is correlated with another if a change in that variable occurs in tandem with a change in the other. It is very important to understand that just because two events are correlated with something doesn't necessarily mean that one thing causes the other. Purchases of mozzarella cheese are correlated with pepperoni sales but people don't buy pepperoni *because* they've bought mozzarella. They buy both because they are making pizza. See also causation.

Cut-off score, *see* decision rule.

Data mining. Data mining came to prominence in the 1980s. It describes the use of computers to find useful information from large quantities of data that are too large for a human to analyze easily on their own. Although data mining includes techniques found in machine learning and artificial intelligence, the term is not very widely used these days.

Data science. The name given to the skill/art of being able combine mathematical (machine learning) knowledge with data and IT skills in a pragmatic way, to deliver practical machine learning-based solutions.

Data scientist. The name given to someone who does data science. Good data scientists focus on delivering useful solutions that work in real-world environments. They don't get too hung up on theory. If it works it works.

Data set. A collection of data available for analysis. Examples of data sets include a spreadsheet containing patient records, details of peoples' credit card transactions and audio recordings of customer calls to a contact center.

Decision bias. One type of bias that can manifest itself in a data driven decision-making system. The system makes biased decisions because the training data used to develop it was also biased. See also, Sample Bias.

Decision rule. Models generate scores; i.e. numeric outputs. Decision rules are used to decide what action to take on the basis of the score. If the score is above a given value (the cut-off) do one thing, otherwise, if the score is below the cut-off, then do something else. For example, when assessing people for a medical condition, only those scoring above the cut-off score; i.e. those with the highest risk of developing the condition, are offered treatment.

Decision tree. A type of predictive model created using an algorithm that recursively segments a population into smaller and smaller groups. Also known as a Classification and Regression Tree or CART (Because they can be used for both classification and regression.)

Deepfake. Something artificial, often created using machine learning techniques, that is passed off as the real thing. For example, creating a fake media clip of a well-known politician or celebrity, and inserting it into a real recording to given the appearance of them saying something that they didn't.

Deep learning. Predictive models based on complex neural networks (or related architectures), containing many artificial neurons spread across many layers. Deep leaning is proving very successful at many complex tasks such as object recognition and language translation.

Development sample. To develop a model, a data scientist will gather a sample of data (training data). The portion of the training data used to train the model is referred to as the development sample. This contrasts with the validation sample, which is used to test the accuracy of the model once training is complete. The development sample needs to contain at least several hundred cases but larger samples lead to better results. Complex AI system use development samples containing millions of examples.

Ensemble. Sometimes, several different models are developed using different methods and different parts of the training data. Each model predicts the same outcome but, because they have been constructed differently, they produce slightly different predictions. The ensemble combines all of the individual predictions together to produce a new prediction that is often more accurate than any of the individual predictions on their own. A simple ensemble can comprise just 3 or 4 models but complex ensembles can contain thousands of separate models.

Evolutionary Computing. A type of computational learning inspired by natural evolution and the principle of "Survival of the fittest." With each iteration of the training algorithm, new "Offspring" solutions (models) are created by randomly combining different parts of the best "Parent" solutions found so far. If the offspring are found to be better than their parents, then the offspring replace them in the next iteration. Small random changes, termed "Mutation," are also applied to introduce new features into the process.

Expert systems. These aim to replicate the deductive reasoning and decision-making capabilities of experts in a particular field. A typical expert system contains two main components. The first is a knowledge base that contains information about the field of interest. The second is an inference engine that, when presented with a set of facts, applies rules to the information contained in the knowledge base to try and determine a suitable answer. For example, given a set of symptoms, what disease is the patient most likely to have?

Feed forward neural network. This is a neural network where the connections are all in one direction from one layer of neurons to the next; i.e. all of the outputs from the neurons in one later provider the inputs to the neurons in the next layer. There are no backward connections or connections to other layers apart from the next one. Most neural networks are feed forward networks.

Forecast horizon. When predicting future events, the forecast horizon refers to the period of time over which the prediction applies. If I build a model to predict the likelihood of people defaulting on their credit cards, then the model will be designed to predict the likelihood of default in say, the next year. However, if I am predicting survival rates for a particular disease, then a forecast horizon of 5 or 10 years may be more appropriate.

General Adversarial Networks (GANs). These comprise two neural networks that use the outputs from each other to learn and improve. One network is trained to create something that appears real, such as an image by a famous painter or soundbite from a celebrity. The second network is trained to identify if the items are real or fake. After many cycles of training, you have a network that can produce things that appear real, but are in fact, completely artificial.

Gartner Hype Cycle. New technologies tend to be over-hyped initially, then under-hyped, before eventually ending up between the two. The Gartner hype cycle captures this behavior very elegantly. More information is available from the Gartner website: .https://www.gartner.com/technology/research/methodologies/hype-cycle.jsp

GDPR. General Data Protection Regulation. (Regulation (EU) 2016/679). The GDPR provides detailed instructions as to how organizations must gather, store and process personal data in EU countries. The scope of the GDPR is the processing of all personal data but it contains some specific clauses relevant to AI technologies. In particular, people have the right to a detailed explanation as to how an automated decision was made if that decision has a significant impact upon them. People also have the right to demand that important decisions are independently reviewed by a human being if they disagree with a decision made by a fully automated system.

General AI. An artificial system that can operate intelligently across many different problem domains, and which can adapt and learn new skills in a similar way to a person can, is described as possessing general intelligence. No AI systems in the world today can be said to possess General AI. See also, Narrow AI.

Gradient descent. A general-purpose algorithm that is widely used to solve optimization problems. In the context of AI/machine learning, gradient descent is used by training algorithms to determine the weights in a model. A commonly used analogy is trying to get to the lowest point in the local landscape as quickly as you can. To do this, you identify the steepest downward path and take a step along it. You repeat the process until you can't get any lower. When building a model deciding which weights to adjust, and by how much, are analogous to determining which direction to go in and how big your step size should be.

Imitation Game (The). The Imitation Game was the name Alan Turing gave to his test to determine if a machine could be classified as intelligent. Today, this is more commonly referred to as the Turning Test. In the Imitation Game / Turing Test, a machine is deemed to be intelligent if a human judge can't distinguish which is the human and which is the machine after engaging both in conversation.

Internet of things (The). Everyday devices such as cars, heating systems and TVs can be connected to the internet and each other. The Internet of Things (IoT) describes these types of connected devices and how they are used. For example, heating systems that predict that they will break down in a few days, find a slot in your smartphone diary and then arrange an engineer visit to fix the problem before it occurs. More and more devices are being seen with internet connectivity, but the IoT concept is still in its infancy.

Linear model. One of the earliest types of predictive model used in in automated decision-making systems. These days, other types of model can often deliver more accurate results, but linear models remain popular because they are easy to understand and use. This means that it is easy to describe why the model delivers a given score, and hence why certain decisions were made. A popular way of representing linear models is in the form of a scorecard, such as the one introduced in Chapter 2.

Machine learning. Machine learning covers a range of algorithms used in artificial intelligence and pattern recognition. Machine learning algorithms are primarily used to find patterns (features) in data. The algorithms used to train (deep) neural networks are one example of machine learning in practice.

Model. A mathematical representation of a real-world system or situation. The model is used to determine how the real-world system would behave under different conditions. In AI, most models predict some type of outcome that is used to make decisions and take actions. See also, predictive model.

Narrow AI. Artificial intelligence applications which are very good at just one or two things, but which can't be applied beyond the problems for which they have been designed. All AI applications in use today can be described as being Narrow AI systems. See also, General AI.

Natural Language Processing (NLP). Algorithms that deal with language; i.e. speech and text processing. A primary aim of NLP is to allow computers to interact with people using everyday language. However, NLP also encompasses language analysis to identify sentiments, emotions and motives. For example, analysis of a twitter feed to identify if a subject is being discussed in a positive or negative way. Another application is detecting fraudulent activity from a criminal's speech patterns.

Neural network. A type of model constructed from a set of interconnected neurons. Neural networks models are very good at capturing complex interactions and non-linarites in data in a way that is analogous to human learning. Deep neural networks (Deep learning/Deep belief networks) are large and complex neural networks, often containing thousands or millions of artificial neurons. These types of models are favored for many advanced AI tasks such as speech recognition and the navigation systems in self-driving vehicles.

Neuron. The key component of a neural network, which is often presented as being analogous to biological neurons in the human brain. In reality, a neuron is a linear model whose score is then subject to a (non-linear) transformation. A neural network can therefore be considered as a set of interconnected linear models and non-linear transformations.

Odds. A popular way to represent the likelihood of an event occurring. The odds of an event are equal to $(1/p) - 1$ where p is the probability of the event. Likewise, the probability is equal to $(1/Odds+1)$. Odds of 1:1 is the same as a probability of 0.5, odds of 2:1 a probability of 0.33, 3:1 a probability of 0.25 and so on.

Over-fitting. This is when an algorithm goes too far in its search for patterns and correlations in the data used to develop a model, resulting in false/non-existent patterns being reported. The result is a model that is very accurate when measured using the training data (the development sample) used to build the model, but in practice performs very poorly when it's used to generate new outcomes using data that has not been used before.

Override rule. Sometimes, you have to carry out a certain action, regardless of the output generated by a model. A predictive model used to target people with offers for beer might predict that some children are very likely to take up the offer. An override rule is therefore put in place to prevent offers being sent to children, regardless of the score generated by the model.

Petabyte. 1,000 Terabytes. Some of the largest commercial databases in existence today (as at 2020) are 100+ petabytes in size. For example, the database of video material maintained by YouTube.

Predictive analytics (PA). This term is used to describe the application of statistical or machine learning techniques to generate predictive models. There is an argument that, for all practical purposes, machine learning and predictive analytics are pretty much the same thing, given that they use the same types of data as inputs, apply the same type of algorithms and generate similar outputs (scores).

Predictive model. A predictive model is the output produced by most machine learning algorithms. The model captures the relationships (correlations) that the training algorithm has discovered. Once a predictive model has been created, it can then be applied to new situations to predict future, or otherwise unknown, events.

Predictive modelling, *see* predictive analytics.

Python. Python has become one of the most popular software packages used for machine learning and the development of AI-based applications. The python software is free and open source, with the user community able to develop new functionality and share it with other users.

Random forest. Random forests combine together the outputs of a large number of decision trees. Each decision tree is created under a slightly different set of conditions and hence, generate different outcomes for a given set of inputs. Random forests are one example of an ensemble model.

Recurrent neural network. A neural network model that can use previous outputs as inputs. These types of network are particularly useful where there are sequential/temporal patterns in data; i.e. the ordering of cases in the development sample is important, such as when predicting text or what is likely to happen next in a video clip.

Regression model. A model that predicts the size or magnitude of something. For example, today's temperature or someone's life expectancy. This is in contrast to classification models that predict the likelihood (probability) that certain events will occur. You may have a classification model to predict the likelihood of someone buying something from your store and a regression model to predict how much they spend.

Reinforcement learning. A machine learning approach where the training algorithm adjusts the model weights based on some measure of success resulting from an action being taken. Each time the model produces an outcome, the quality of that outcome is assessed. The training algorithm then adjusts the model weights depending on how successful it was. Reinforcement learning is viewed as more similar to the way people learn than other types of machine learning; i.e. supervised learning.

Response (choice) model. A classification model used predict the likelihood of someone choosing a given option. This type of model is widely used in marketing to determine what products or services a customer is likely to choose (buy) so that they can be targeted with relevant offers.

Sample bias (Sampling bias). This is when the training data does not contain a representative sample of the population. Common sample biases include under-representation of certain ethnicities, genders, ages and disabilities.

Score. Each output generated by a model is usually a number (a score). For a classification model, each score represents the probability of an event occurring e.g. the probability that someone will prove to be a good hire or the likelihood that the object in a picture is a cat. With regression models, the scores predict the magnitude of something. For example, what the temperature will be this time next week or how much disposable income someone has.

Scorecard. A popular way to present linear models, that is easy for non-experts to understand. The main benefit of a scorecard is that it is additive. The model score is calculated by simply adding up the points that apply. Multiplication, division or other more complex arithmetic is not required.

Sentiment analysis. Techniques that are used for extracting information about peoples' attitude towards things. For example, sentiment analysis can be used to analyze responses to a blog post to see if readers had a positive or negative view of the opinions expressed in the post. In artificial intelligence, sentiment analysis is used to extract information from text or speech that is then used to build predictive models or derive clusters.

Supervised learning. The application of machine learning where each case in the development sample has an associated outcome that one wants to predict. The cases are said to be "Labelled." An example of supervised learning in target marketing is where each customer's response to marketing activity is known (they either responded or they didn't). The model generated by the algorithm is then optimized to predict if customers will respond to marketing or not. In practice, most machine learning approaches are examples of supervised learning.

Terabyte. 1,000 gigabytes. One terabyte of storage can hold the text for around one million books or about 250 hours of HD video. A typical laptop, that you can by in 2020, has between 0.25 and 1 terabytes of storge.

Threshold, *see* Decision rule.

Training. Training is a term used to describe the process of iteratively refining a model to improve its accuracy. See also, training algorithm.

Training algorithm. A machine learning algorithm used to determine the structure and/or weights in a model. The term is most widely used to describe algorithms that determine the weights for neural network models. The algorithm adjusts the weights in the network with the aim of optimizing the network's performance. The training algorithm terminates after a fixed number of iterations or when no further significant improvements in model performance are obtained.

Training data, *see* Development sample.

Turing test, *see* Imitation Game

Unsupervised learning. The application of machine learning when the training data doesn't contain labels (outcomes). Unsupervised algorithms typically group cases with similar characteristics (features) together. An example of unsupervised learning is an organization wanting to come up with an ad placement policy for an expensive luxury product, where no information exists about customers' purchasing history. Clustering is applied to group similar customers together based on their age, income, gender etc. The ad placement strategy is then targeted at individuals within clusters where the average income is high, rather than clusters with lower incomes.

Validation sample. An independent data set used to test the performance of a model after it has been constructed. The validation sample should be completely separate from the development sample and should not be used by the training algorithm to determine the structure of the model. Using a validation sample is important because machine learning sometimes reports over-optimistic results if its performance is measured using the data used to build it. To put it another way, if you evaluate a model using the original training data it can appear to be more predictive than it actually is. See also, over-fitting

Variable. A data item containing information about something. For example, someone's age or income, how fast a plane is flying, the temperature today and so on.

Weak AI, *see* Narrow AI.

About the Author

Steven Finlay has been doing stuff with data and machine learning for a couple of decades now. He's done a lot of technical nerdy stuff in his time, but these days, his focus is on the bigger picture and broader issues associated with implementing new technologies. This is so that they are used successfully for the benefit of business and society. He holds a PhD in predictive modelling and is an honorary research fellow at Lancaster University in the UK.

Steve has previously been employed by one of the UK's leading banks to manage their inventory of credit risk models, has developed machine learning approaches for the UK government and worked for a number of consultancy groups and a credit reference agency. He is currently Head of Analytics for Computershare Loan Services (CLS) in the UK.

Steve has published a number of practically focused books about machine learning, artificial intelligence and financial services. His other books include:

- *Artificial Intelligence for Everyone*. Relativistic.
- *Artificial Intelligence and Machine Learning for Business. A No-Nonsense Guide to Data Driven Technologies*. Relativistic.
- *Predictive Analytics, Data Mining and Big Data. Myths, Misconceptions and Methods*. Palgrave Macmillan.
- *Credit Scoring, Response Modeling and Insurance Rating. A Practical Guide to Forecasting Consumer Behavior*. Palgrave Macmillan.

- *Dice Role Tables*. Relativistic
- *The Management of Consumer Credit. Theory and Practice.* Palgrave Macmillan.
- *Consumer Credit Fundamentals.* Palgrave Macmillan.

Notes

[1] Alan M. Turing. (1950). "Computing Machinery and Intelligence." Mind 49, p. 433-460.

[2] There is some debate as to what constitutes a pass and under what conditions. For example, how the judge is selected and how many and what type of questions they can ask. In my view, the machine would need to be able to pass the majority of the time, when questioned at length about a wide range of topics by a person of at least average intelligence. A one-off fluke win would not count in my book.

[3] John R. Searle. (1980). "Minds, brains, and programs." Behavioral and Brain Sciences 3 (3), p. 417-457. Also see the arguments in the 2019 book by Christof Koch: "The Feeling of Life Itself: Why consciousness is widespread but can't be computed," as well as those by Roger Penrose in his books: "The Emperor's New Mind: Concerning Computers, Minds, and the Laws of Physics" and "Shadows of The Mind: A Search for the Missing Science of Consciousness."

[4] https://www.captionbot.ai/, accessed 23/06/2019.

[5] https://thispersondoesnotexist.com/, accessed 02/01/2020.

[6] https://www.bostondynamics.com/robots, accessed 15/11/2019

[7] Douglas Heaven. (2019). "AI can't see things from another view." New Scientist 241(3221), p. 15.

[8] Chris Baraniuk. (2019). "One of these is a power drill." New Scientist 242(3227). New Scientist, p. 34-7.

[9] Rachel Metz. (2018). "Microsoft's neo-Nazi sexbot was a great lesson for makers of AI assistants." MIT Technology Review. https://www.technologyreview.com/s/610634/microsofts-neo-nazi-sexbot-was-a-great-lesson-for-makers-of-ai-assistants/, accessed 06/01/2020.

---

[10] Microsoft Azure. https://azure.microsoft.com/en-gb/services/machine-learning/?&wt.mc_id=AID529440_SEM

[11] Google Cloud Prediction API. https://cloud.google.com/prediction/

[12] Alexa Voice Service (AVS) https://developer.amazon.com/public/solutions/alexa/alexa-voice-service/getting-started-with-the-alexa-voice-service, accessed 30/03/2019.

[13] That is not to say that many people won't all receive the same credit score, but that the route to arrive at that score, via the set of characteristics used to calculate it, may be different for everyone.

[14] It's all to do with air pressure. The lower the air pressure the lower the boiling point of water. A rough rule of thumb is that the boiling point drops by one degree centigrade for each 1,000 feet (300 metres). At the top of Everest (28,029 feet) the boiling point of water is only about 72 degrees. This would not make a very good cup of tea.

[15] Steven Finlay. (2012). Credit Scoring, Response Modeling and Insurance Rating: A Practical Guide to Forecasting Consumer Behaviour. Palgrave Macmillan. 2nd Edn, p.8.

[16] Body Mass Index (BMI) is calculated as a person's weight in kilograms divided by their height in metres squared. For someone who is 180cm tall and weighs 80kg their body mass index is: $80/(1.8 * 1.8) = 24.69$. In the UK, a BMI of 19-25 is considered normal. A BMI under 19 indicates a person may be underweight. 25-30 indicates that someone is likely to be overweight and more than 30 obese. Note that BMI is only a guide, and other factors such as build, age and muscle mass are also important. Some athletes would be classified as overweight using BMI due to having more than the average amount of muscle mass.

[17] In terms of how well an automated loan granting system, based on a scorecard, performs then the general findings are that they can outperform trained human underwriters by 20-30% By replacing human underwriters with the scorecard, a loan company can expect to see a reduction in bad debts of 20-30% and every dollar of reduced bad debt is another dollar on the bottom line. Once organizations understood the potential benefits, credit scoring was a no brainer.

[18] This assumes that the future will be like the past; i.e. a customer today will behave in a similar way to customers previously. This is a pretty big assumption to make, but generally holds true in very many situations.

[19] Rosenblatt, F. (1958). "The perceptron: A probabilistic model for information storage and organisation in the brain." Psychological Review 65.

[20] Their full title is Artificial Neural Network or ANN, but these days, most people just use the term Neural Network.

[21] Rumelhart, D. E., Hinton, G. E. and Williams, R. J. (1986). "Learning representations by back-propagating errors." Nature 323(6088).

[22] For things such as employment status, indicators represent each option. 1 = employed, 2 = retired so on. For example, if Weight2 was say, 0.75, then a retired applicant would contribute 1.5 to the initial score (0.75 * 2). This approach can be used if the values represent a scale, but if the data represents a category, then a more common approach is to create a separate 0/1 flag for each condition. There would be one flag for employed, one flag for retired, one for home maker and so on.

[23] Forcing all the scores to lie in the same range is not absolutely essential, but is usually deemed to be good practice, particularly for classification problems.

[24] It can be demonstrated that the outputs from a neuron like this and a scorecard model are equivalent.

[25] One exception to this is when the final output needs to align with a defined range for business or legal reasons. For example, many credit scores predict default probabilities (in the range 0 to 1) but are scaled to be in the range 0 – 1,000. There is no technical reason why credit scores need to be scaled in this way, but over the years, it has become standard practice in the credit industry. Similarly, if the output is predicting a quantity, such as customer spend, then you would want the output to align to actual spend, rather than being constrained to lie within a fixed range.

[26] This works particularly well for problem such as image recognition. This is because standard neural networks, where all the inputs are provided to every neuron in the first layer, do not account for the spatial nature of images. For example, the pixels at the top left of an image often have no relation to the pixels at the bottom right. Therefore, it makes sense not to provide all inputs to every neuron.

[27] The models don't have to be neural networks but, in nearly all practical applications, neural network models are used due to their superior performance.

[28] There are lots of different flavours of GANs – some use random inputs as I've described, but some types of GAN are designed to transform inputs rather than create something from scratch. For example, to transform a photograph you've taken on your phone into the style of a painting by a famous artist. In this case, the inputs would be your photograph and the output would be the new image.

[29] https://thispersondoesnotexist.com/

[30] Will Knight. (2019). "Amazon Has Developed an AI Fashion Designer." MIT Technology Review. https://www.technologyreview.com/s/608668/amazon-has-developed-an-ai-fashion-designer/, accessed 25/05/2020.

[31] The shape of a protein is key to determining how it will interact with other substances. The task here is to determine the shape, when given a list of the protein's component parts. In theory, you could go through every possible configuration to find the actual shape of a given protein, but there are so many possible combinations that to explore them all could take trillions of years using the most powerful computers available.

[32] There are also forms of supervised clustering. One such example is the popular K-nearest neighbour approach. When a prediction is required for a new case, the algorithm finds the K cases in the development sample that are most similar to it. The model score is calculated as the proportion of the K cases which displayed the behavior (outcome). If K=200, then the algorithm would find the 200 cases most similar to the case a prediction is required for. If say, 18 out of the 200 cases display the behavior, then the score is 0.09 (18/200). What value of K to use is usually determined by trial and error.

[33] 956,390 papers were added to the medline database in 2019. https://www.nlm.nih.gov/bsd/stats/cit_added.html, accessed 26/05/2020.

[34] In chess, each piece is assigned a value aligned to how important it is. A pawn is assigned a value of 1. A bishop is considered three times more valuable than a pawn, and therefore, has a value of 3. A rook (castle) has a value of 5 and so on. Consequently, a simple view of the game can be determined by summing up the value of each players' pieces remaining on the board. An actual assessment of who is winning during a game is of course far more complex than this. All advanced chess programs consider the position of the pieces as being just as important, if not more so.

However, a simple points based measure of success is very easy to understand and calculate.

[35] Knapton, S. and Watson, L. (2017). "Entire human chess knowledge learned and surpassed by DeepMind's AlphaZero in four hours." The Telegraph. https://www.telegraph.co.uk/science/2017/12/06/entire-human-chess-knowledge-learned-surpassed-deepminds-alphazero/, accessed 11/07/2019.

[36] Another weakness of reinforcement learning is the cost of failure during the training process. If you embed a reinforcement learning algorithm into an organization's recruitment policy, for example, then you are going to get a lot of terrible hires initially which is going to cause all sorts of problems.

[37] Steven Finlay. (2017). "We Should Be as Scared of Artificial Intelligence as Elon Musk Is." Fortune. https://fortune.com/2017/08/18/elon-musk-artificial-intelligence-risk/, accessed 18/11/2019.

[38] BBC News. (2019). "China due to introduce face scans for mobile users." BBC News. https://www.bbc.co.uk/news/world-asia-china-50587098, accessed 22/12/2019.

[39] Leo Kelion. (2018). "Facebook gives users trustworthiness score." BBC News. https://www.bbc.co.uk/news/technology-45257894, accessed 26/05/2020.

[40] When I say appropriately, this includes things such as people not being forced into actions just because someone else says it's good for them. For example, the right not be penalized if they subsequently don't follow the health advice that they are recommended.

[41] Robert Booty. (2019). "Benefits system automation could plunge claimants deeper into poverty." The Guardian. https://www.theguardian.com/technology/2019/oct/14/fears-rise-in-benefits-system-automation-could-plunge-claimants-deeper-into-poverty, accessed 26/10/2019.

[42] Luke Rhinehart. (1956). The Dice Man. William Morrow. In the book Luke, a psychiatrist, advocates a philosophy of making all important life decisions via the role of the dice.

[43] Somon Maybin (2016). "How maths can get you locked up." BBC News. https://www.bbc.co.uk/news/magazine-37658374, accessed 03/12/2019.

[44] Matthew Wall. (2019). "Biased and wrong? Facial recognition tech in the dock." BBC News. https://www.bbc.co.uk/news/business-48842750, accessed 01/12/2019.

[45] Adam Vaughan. (2019). "UK launched passport photo checker it knew would fail with dark skin." New Scientist. https://www.newscientist.com/article/2219284-uk-launched-passport-photo-checker-it-knew-would-fail-with-dark-skin/, accessed 28/10/2019.

[46] This example is adapted from: Steven Finlay. (2014). Predictive Analytics, Data Mining and Big Data. Myths, Misconceptions and Methods. Palgrave Macmillan, p. 92.

[47] This is what most companies are obliged to do under their Articles of Association. The Articles of Association describe what the company's aims are; i.e. what the company is set up to do. Often, this includes maximizing the return for shareholders and owners, but can include other objectives such as supporting charities or engaging in community action.

[48] Michael J. Rosenfeld, Reuben J. Thomas, and Sonia Hausen. (2019). "Disintermediating your friends: How online dating in the United States displaces other ways of meeting." Proceedings of the National Academy of Sciences of the United States of America. 116(36).

[49] i.e. they decide what the objective is for the training algorithms to use in terms of what constitutes "good" compatibility between two individuals.

[50] The precise model algorithms used will differ by purpose but the training process employed to develop the models will be similar. The key difference is the different training data used and what the model is tasked to predict. Therefore, one tends to see the same general principles being applied in terms of how recommendations are generated by the resulting models, regardless of the type of product or service.

[51] There were other important factors as well, such as globalization and the transfer of a lot of manufacturing capacity to developing nations where it was cheaper to produce things.

[52] Mark Overton. (2011). "Agricultural Revolution in England 1500 – 1850." BBC. http://www.bbc.co.uk/history/british/empire_seapower/agricultural_revolution_01.shtml, accessed 09/08/2019.

[53] The 22% and 1% figures are only loosely comparable, given factors such as imports and exports, and changes in working patterns.

[54] Frey, C. and Osborne, M. (2013). "THE FUTURE OF EMPLOYMENT: HOW SUSCEPTIBLE ARE JOBS TO COMPUTERISATION." Technological Forecasting and Social Change 114.

[55] The paper does not give a definitive date but states: "According to our estimate, 47 percent of total US employment is in the high risk category, meaning that associated occupations are potentially automatable over some unspecified number of years, perhaps a decade or two." Which gets us to somewhere around 2030-2035.

[56] Nedelkoska, L. and G. Quintini. (2018), "Automation, skills use and training.", OECD Social, Employment and Migration Working Papers, No. 202, OECD Publishing, Paris, http://dx.doi.org/10.1787/2e2f4eea-en., accessed 06/05/2018.

[57] 2010 is rather arbitrary, but concerns about artificial intelligence were certainly being raised many years before I wrote this book. For example, see the 2011 book: "Race Against The Machine: How the Digital Revolution is Accelerating Innovation, Driving Productivity, and Irreversibly Transforming Employment and the Economy" by Erik Brynjolfsson and Andrew McAfee.

[58] Why have I used the US employment rate? Because the US is the largest economy in the world (In terms of GDP) and it's also where a significant proportion of the current wave of new AI technology is being developed and deployed. That's not to say a lot isn't going on in other countries, but the US is probably the single most representative one.

[59] United States Department of Labor. Bureau of Labor Statistics. Series LNS14000000.

[60] United States Department of Labor. Bureau of Labor Statistics. NonFarm Business Sector. Labour Productivity. August 2019 press release.

[61] Zoe Thomas (2020). "Coronavirus: Will Covid-19 speed up the use of robots to replace human workers?" BBC. https://www.bbc.co.uk/news/technology-52340651 accessed 20/05/2020.

[62] For example, a survey of 590 business leaders undertaken by KPMG in 2019, reported that only 14% expected to make people who were displaced by intelligent automation redundant. Most were seeking to retrain or redeploy people. KPMG. (2019). "Easing the pressure points: The State of Intelligent Automation." KPMG, p.27. https://assets.kpmg/content/dam/kpmg/xx/pdf/2019/03/easing-pressure-points-the-state-of-intelligent-automation.pdf, accessed 06/09/2019.

[63] In the book: "Alice Through the Looking Glass" by Lewis Carrol, the Red Queen's race refers to Alice making no apparent progress to move forward, no matter however fast she ran. A general interpretation is that this is Carrol's analogy to real life, in which we exert all our efforts just to maintain our relative position in society. Take your foot of the gas and you'll be left behind.

[64] Brian O'Neill. (2019). "Failure rates for analytics, AI and big data projects =85% - Yikes!" Designing for Analytics. https://designingforanalytics.com/resources/failure-rates-for-analytics-bi-iot-and-big-data=/-projects-85-yikes/, accessed 26/05/2020.

[65] Various different surveys tend to agree in terms of the type of jobs and tasks that are most and least at risk of automation.

[66] The formulation of utilitarianism is attributed to the British philosophers Jeremy Bentham (1748 - 1832) and John Stuart Mill (1806 – 73).

[67] Kant termed this the "Categorical Imperative."

[68] John Locke (1632-1714) proposed a list of rights that included the right to life, liberty and property for all. These rights were subsequently incorporated into the American Declaration of Independence and the French Declaration of the Rights of Man in 1776 and 1789 respectively. Today, the list of basic human rights has grown to include a host of other things, such as the right to free speech and religious freedom. But where do these rights come from? One view is that they are 'God given.' However, an alternative view is that we should move beyond the idea that society merely protects the existing rights of individuals to one where we define rights as those that should be granted by a just society (John Rawls 1921-2002). Human rights can be considered complementary to Kant's ideas of duty and respect for individuals. For example, I can argue that employees have the right to receive a living wage for their work while employers have a duty to provide workers with a decent salary.

[69] Paul Finlay. (2000). Strategic Management. An Introduction to Business and Corporate Strategy. Pearson Education Limited, p.75.

[70] The Equal Credit Opportunity Act (ECOA) was passed to prevent unfair discrimination against certain groups when applying for credit. As a result, credit granting decisions cannot be made wholly or partly on the grounds of race, religion, gender, nation of origin or marital status. Age can be used to a degree, but not in a negative way; i.e. to decline a credit application.

[71] European Council of Europe. 1981. "Treaty 108. Convention for the Protection of Individuals with regard to Automatic Processing of Personal Data."

[72] The GDPR (Article 9) defines this type of data as "special category data." This includes personal data revealing racial or ethnic origin, political opinions, religious or philosophical beliefs; trade union membership; genetic data; biometric data (where used for identification purposes); data concerning health, and data concerning a person's sex life or their sexual orientation. There are a number of situations where this type of data can be used, for example where an individual has intentionally made the information public.

[73] For example, the Consumer Privacy Act (AB 375) that came into force in California on 01/01/2020, which has some similar provisions to those found in the GDPR.

[74] GDPR Article 5(1) requires personal data to be processed lawfully, fairly and in a transparent manner. See also Recital 60.

[75] GDPR Articles 13 and 14.

[76] ICO. (2019). "ICO and The Alan Turing Institute open consultation on first piece of AI guidance." https://ico.org.uk/about-the-ico/news-and-events/news-and-blogs/2019/12/ico-and-the-alan-turing-institute-open-consultation-on-first-piece-of-ai-guidance/, accessed 07/12/2019.

[77] The "Three laws of robotics" that Asimov put forward in his Robot novels where: (1) "A robot may not injure a human being or, through inaction, allow a human being to come to harm." (2) "A robot must obey orders given it by human beings except where such orders would conflict with the First Law." And (3) "A robot must protect its own existence as long as such protection does not conflict with the First or Second Law."

[78] This is a version of Amara's Law, formulated by the American futurologist Roy Charles Amara (1925 – 2007). This stated that: "We tend to overestimate the effect of a technology in the short run and underestimate the effect in the long run."

[79] For example, Elon Musk was reported to have been talking about autonomous cross-country trips being available in 2017. General Motors promised us that self-driving rides would be available in 2019 and Ford was talking about 2021, which now looks unlikely. Matt McFarland. (2019). "Self-driving cars: Hype-filled decade ends on sobering note." CNN.

https://edition.cnn.com/2019/12/18/tech/self-driving-cars-decade/index.html, accessed 02/01/2020.

[80] This is part of a quote attributed to Mark Zuckerberg which goes: "Move fast and break things. Unless you are breaking stuff, you are not moving fast enough."

[81] Yves Mersch. (2019). "Money and private currencies - reflections on Libra." Bank of International Settlements. https://www.bis.org/review/r190902a.htm, accessed 02/01/2020.

[82] This is a good test. It may be relatively easy to create a new "Crypto-currency" and use it to exchange goods and services, but it's a very different thing for it to become recognised as a universal medium of exchange that has the backing of governments and central banks.

[83] The Guardian. (2018). "Amazon ditched AI recruiting tool that favored men for technical jobs." The Guardian. https://www.theguardian.com/technology/2018/oct/10/amazon-hiring-ai-gender-bias-recruiting-engine, accessed 04/01/2020.

www.ingramcontent.com/pod-product-compliance
Lightning Source LLC
LaVergne TN
LVHW052303060326
832902LV00021B/3688